LANGUAGE AND LITERACY SERIES

Dorothy S. Strickland, FOUNDING EDITOR

Celia Genishi and Donna E. Alvermann, SERIES EDITORS

ADVISORY BOARD: Richard Allington, Kathryn Au, Bernice Cullinan, Colette Daiute, Anne Haas Dyson, Carole Edelsky, Shirley Brice Heath, Connie Juel, Susan Lytle, Timothy Shanahan

* Volumes with an asterisk following the title are a part of the NCRLL set: Approaches to Language and Literacy Research, edited by JoBeth Allen and Donna E. Alvermann.

(Continued)

Give Them Poetry! A Guide for Sharing Poetry with Children K–8
GLENNA SLOAN

The Brothers and Sisters Learn to Write: Popular Literacies in Childhood and School Cultures
ANNE HAAS DYSON

"Just Playing the Part": Engaging Adolescents in Drama and Literacy
CHRISTOPHER WORTHMAN

The Testing Trap: How State Writing Assessments Control Learning
GEORGE HILLOCKS, JR.

School's Out! Bridging Out-of-School Literacies with Classroom Practice
GLYNDA HULL & KATHERINE SCHULTZ, EDS.

Reading Lives: Working-Class Children and Literacy Learning
DEBORAH HICKS

Inquiry Into Meaning: An Investigation of Learning to Read, Revised Edition
EDWARD CHITTENDEN & TERRY SALINGER, WITH ANNE M. BUSSIS

"Why Don't They Learn English?" Separating Fact from Fallacy in the U.S. Language Debate
LUCY TSE

Conversational Borderlands: Language and Identity in an Alternative Urban High School
BETSY RYMES

Inquiry-Based English Instruction
RICHARD BEACH & JAMIE MYERS

The Best for Our Children: Critical Perspectives on Literacy for Latino Students
MARÍA DE LA LUZ REYES & JOHN J. HALCÓN, EDS.

Language Crossings
KAREN L. OGULNICK, ED.

What Counts as Literacy?
MARGARET GALLEGO & SANDRA HOLLINGSWORTH, EDS.

Critical Encounters in High School English: Teaching Literary Theory to Adolescents
DEBORAH APPLEMAN

Beginning Reading and Writing
DOROTHY S. STRICKLAND & LESLEY M. MORROW, EDS.

Reading for Meaning
BARBARA M. TAYLOR, MICHAEL F. GRAVES, & PAUL VAN DEN BROEK, EDS.

Writing in the Real World
ANNE BEAUFORT

Young Adult Literature and the New Literary Theories
ANNA O. SOTER

Literacy Matters
ROBERT P. YAGELSKI

Children's Inquiry: Using Language to Make Sense of the World
JUDITH WELLS LINDFORS

Close to Home: Oral and Literate Practices in a Transnational Mexicano Community
JUAN C. GUERRA

Authorizing Readers: Resistance and Respect in the Teaching of Literature
PETER J. RABINOWITZ & MICHAEL W. SMITH

On the Brink: Negotiating Literature and Life with Adolescents
SUSAN HYNDS

Life at the Margins: Literacy, Language, and Technology in Everyday Life
JULIET MERRIFIELD, ET AL.

Literacy for Life: Adult Learners, New Practices
HANNA ARLENE FINGERET & CASSANDRA DRENNON

The Book Club Connection
SUSAN I. MCMAHON & TAFFY E. RAPHAEL, EDS., WITH VIRGINIA J. GOATLEY & LAURA S. PARDO

Until We Are Strong Together: Women Writers in the Tenderloin
CAROLINE E. HELLER

Restructuring Schools for Linguistic Diversity
OFELIA B. MIRAMONTES, ADEL NADEAU, & NANCY L. COMMINS

Writing Superheroes
ANNE HAAS DYSON

Opening Dialogue
MARTIN NYSTRAND, ET AL.

Just Girls
MARGARET J. FINDERS

The First R
MICHAEL F. GRAVES, PAUL VAN DEN BROEK, & BARBARA M. TAYLOR, EDS.

Exploring Blue Highways
JOBETH ALLEN, MARILYNN CARY, & LISA DELGADO

Envisioning Literature
JUDITH A. LANGER

Teaching Writing as Reflective Practice
GEORGE HILLOCKS, JR.

Talking Their Way into Science
KAREN GALLAS

Whole Language Across the Curriculum
SHIRLEY C. RAINES, ED.

Dramatizing Literature in Whole Language Classrooms, Second Edition
JOHN WARREN STEWIG & CAROL BUEGE

The Languages of Learning
KAREN GALLAS

Partners in Learning
CAROL LYONS, GAY SU PINNELL, & DIANE DEFORD

Social Worlds of Children Learning to Write in an Urban Primary School
ANNE HAAS DYSON

Inside/Outside
MARILYN COCHRAN-SMITH & SUSAN L. LYTLE

Whole Language Plus
Courtney B. Cazden

Learning to Read
G. BRIAN THOMPSON & TOM NICHOLSON, EDS.

Engaged Reading
JOHN T. GUTHRIE & DONNA E. ALVERMANN

Children, Language, and Literacy

Diverse Learners in Diverse Times

Celia Genishi
Anne Haas Dyson

Teachers College
Columbia University
New York and London

National Association for the
Education of Young Children
Washington, DC

Drawings of children on cover were created by Tionna, Miguel, and Alicia.

Published simultaneously by Teachers College Press, 1234 Amsterdam Avenue, New York, NY 10027, and the National Association for the Education of Young Children (NAEYC), 1313 L Street NW, Suite 500, Washington, DC 20005.

Library of Congress Cataloging-in-Publication Data

Genishi, Celia, 1944–
    Children, language, and literacy : diverse learners in diverse times / Celia Genishi, Anne
        Haas Dyson.
            p. cm. — (Language and literacy series)
            Includes bibliographical references and index.
            ISBN 978-0-8077-4974-6 (pbk. : alk. paper)
            ISBN 978-0-8077-4975-3 (hardcover : alk. paper)
        1. Language arts (Elementary)—United States. 2. English language—Social aspects—
    United States. 3. Multicultural education—United States 4. Children—Language.
    5. Early childhood education—United States. I. Dyson, Anne Haas. II. Title.
    LB1576.G374 2009
    372.6–dc22   2008055103

ISBN 978–0-8077–4974–6 (paper)
ISBN 978–0-8077–4975–3 (cloth)

NAEYC Item # 349

Printed on acid-free paper
Manufactured in the United States of America

16   15   14   13   12   11   10   09   8   7   6   5   4   3   2   1

To our students, each and every one,
young and grown up,
near and far
in time and space

Contents

Acknowledgments

The finishing touch of the long, lived experience of creating a book is the pleasurable process of saying thank you—a process that is ultimately reduced to a small number of, we hope, meaning-laden words. Authors usually lead up to a final paragraph, acknowledging the person or people who are closest to the heart. In the case of this book, we have a list of people who were all close to the heart—of both the book and our literal hearts. Some were indispensable to the shape of the book or the studies we incorporate below. We gratefully acknowledge our debts:

In Chapter 1 we thank most sincerely Sal Vascellaro, a member of the graduate faculty at the Bank Street College of Education, for alerting us to Miriam Cohen's book, *First Grade Takes a Test,* which set us on the path to envisioning the structure of our book.

Beginning in Chapter 2, we express heartfelt thanks to the dedicated and caring "Mrs. Kay," in whose lively classroom we found Tionna and other children featured throughout our book. The project in Mrs. Kay's room benefitted enormously from the good-humored assistance of Yanan Fan, California State University–San Francisco, and Tambra Jackson, University of South Carolina–Columbia. Much appreciation is due as well to the Spencer Foundation, which generously funded the work in Mrs. Kay's and Donna Yung-Chan's room (and is not, of course, responsible for our perspectives), and also to Michigan State University and Dean Carole Ames for gratefully received faculty funds (and professional enthusiasm).

The studies described in Chapter 3 relied on the indispensable collaboration and always enjoyable company of Ariela Zycherman, a doctoral candidate in the Teachers College (hereafter referred to as TC) program in Applied Anthropology, Department of International and Transcultural Studies; Ysaaca Axelrod and Lorraine Falchi, doctoral students in the Department of Curriculum and Teaching, TC, Columbia; Susan Stires, of the graduate faculty, the

Bank Street College of Education; and Donna Yung-Chan, now a kindergarten teacher, and Rosie Young, 1st-grade teacher at P.S. 1 in New York City. We relied equally on Marilyn Barnwell, with her gift for enabling good work, and the welcoming teachers on her pre-kindergarten staff, here called Fran, Lana, Pat, and Dominga. We thank the administration of TC for a generous research leave and much appreciated funding for the Head Start study.

An added word about naming in the book: When teachers asked us to use their actual names, we use their first and last names to introduce them. Thereafter the name their children used with them is used. Pseudonyms are given to children, except for the children in Rosie Young's and Donna Yung-Chan's rooms.

In Chapter 4 we tip our hats to Kim Parker, doctoral student in the Department of Curriculum & Instruction at the University of Illinois, Urbana–Champaign (UIUC), who called our attention to the N. Scott Momaday story that inspired our discussion of language and play.

In Chapter 5, we affectionately acknowledge the thoughtful and just plain fun "Mrs. Bee," who allowed us access to her kindergartners. The work in Mrs. Bee's room continues to date with the much appreciated help of Sophie Dewayani, doctoral student in the Department of Curriculum and Instruction at UIUC. Thanks are also due to UIUC's College of Education, which provided essential funds for beginning the work.

In Chapter 6 we very warmly thank early childhood special educators at TC and elsewhere and most especially colleagues in the Integrated Early Childhood teacher education program at TC, who provided information about young children with special needs for this chapter and who have helped over the years to blur the boundary between "general" and "special" education. We take responsibility, though, for interpretations herein about boundaries and relationships between the traditionally separate fields. We also thank Joanne Frantz, Stephanie Rottmayer, and Jan Waters of the School for Young Children, Columbus, Ohio; and Min Hong, New York City Department of Education, for their invaluable assessment stories and for many years of story sharing and friendship. Thank you, too, to Virginia Casper, a member of the graduate faculty at the Bank Street College of Education; and Rachel Theilheimer, professor of early childhood education at the Borough of Manhattan Community College, the City University of New York, for agreeing to share assessment stories, parts of which appear in their forthcoming book.

We enthusiastically applaud the able and cheerful assistance with the manuscript of Sherene Alexander, Director of Academic Administration, Curriculum and Teaching, TC; Nikisha Blackmon, doctoral student in Curriculum and Instruction at UIUC; Ida Esannason, academic secretary in Curriculum and Teaching; Lia Kamitsis, master's student in Counseling Psychology at TC; and Felicia Smart-Williams, department secretary in Curriculum and Teaching.

We owe more than the usual heaps of thanks to the staff at Teachers College Press. This is a book with a long developmental history, so long we have lost count of the appropriate units of time. Carol Chambers Collins, formerly the acquisitions editor of the Language and Literacy series, lent her unswerving and humor-laced support as the ideas in the book were in the phases of infancy and early childhood. Meg Lemke, the current acquisition editor of the series, stepped in with abundant energy and patient support toward the end of adolescence and the beginning of adulthood, if a book all about young children can ever be said to grow into adulthood. Susan Liddicoat served as developmental editor. With her depth of knowledge about early childhood education—and amazing editorial speed—she helped us write a clearer, more transparent book. And for rounding out the book's adulthood, we thank Shannon Waite who expeditiously and kindly supervised the production process.

We also want to offer with deep affection a generic, yet from-the-bottom-of-our-hearts, thank you to the children and families portrayed in these pages and to every student we have ever encountered who has shown an interest in our work and allowed us to share stories, in class and out of class, about children and their teachers. Our stories are your stories.

Our respective families are always close to our hearts. We especially want to acknowledge Richard Hiroshi Genishi, Celia's father; and Athleen W. Haas, Anne's mother, who continue to animate our days. They have lived through diverse times—interesting economic, historic, and cultural eras. Through our lives with them and our other much-loved family members we have learned that individuals are diverse "in time." They develop at their own tempos following their own inner clocks, like the children you will meet in the pages of this book.

And diverse times are something that the two of us know about through the long development of this book. We also have our individual inner clocks, which were sometimes in sync and sometimes out of sync as each of us worked on multiple writing projects. Through the years, though, we kept alive the passions underlying the book—about children, what makes sense to and for them, and how children must all have opportunities to develop their language(s) and literacies, their sense of agency and of possibilities and, in the end, their sociolinguistic flexibility as their worlds expand. So, finally, we acknowledge everyone's longtime support in helping us express ourselves through the pages of this book—and we happily acknowledge the keystone of our abiding friendship over many years upon which this book rests. A toast and a huge thank you to all!

1. Children, Language, and Literacy Now

When Children Are Diverse and Practices Are Not

—

We begin by inviting you into a fictional 1st-grade classroom, where a diverse group of children and their teacher live through their school days together in relative harmony. As told by Miriam Cohen in *First Grade Takes a Test* (1980/2006), the story is this: A woman from the principal's office comes by the 1st grade one day with a pile of tests. The teacher (who is unnamed), in as kind and clear a way as possible, tells the children how to take the test, with its little squares next to multiple-choice answers. During the test some children are unaccustomed to the silence of the testing situation and tell the teacher what the real answers are. For example, faced with the question "What do rabbits eat?", George tells her that rabbits eat carrots even though "carrots" is not one of the answers on the test. So George carefully draws a carrot on the test.

Too quickly, time passes, and the teacher says, "Time is up!" All the children think they did not do well on the test, except for Anna Maria. She declares that the test was easy, so in a few days she is "disappeared," promoted to the special class down the hall. Some time passes again, this time a few days, and children seem cranky, calling each other "dummy." The teacher, knowing that this name characterizes none of her children, reminds them that the test did *not* tell them what they were *able* to do, like build things, read books, make pictures, and help their friends. By the end of the week, civility is restored when Anna Maria returns, having been a daily drop-in visitor to her 1st-grade room anyway. She had jobs there that only she knew how to do. At the end of the story the teacher says, "It's good to be together again. We don't need a test to tell us that!" (Cohen, 1980/2006, n.p.).

Unfortunately, this idyllically sweet story describes very few present-day 1st-grade classrooms in the United States. So the teacher's insights are poignant

1

reminders of what is missing in many schools in the early childhood and primary grade range: time to build, draw, read a good book, solve problems, develop
friendships—in short, time to acknowledge the things each person is able to do,
extending way beyond reading and math skills.

Miriam Cohen's slice of 1st-grade life is, sad to say, out of date, as kindergarten appears to become the new first grade and pre-kindergarten (pre-K) becomes
the new kindergarten. Test anxiety is now a concern in many a pre-K, both public
and private (Hu, 2008). So in this book we recognize today's challenges of working in classrooms with young children, while, like the fictitious 1st-grade teacher,
we foreground what children are able to do. And one of the things almost all
children can do with ease is learn and use language, a stunning accomplishment
that we too often take for granted.

For a pre-kindergartner or primary-grade student to come to the point of
having conversations, much had to happen physically, cognitively, emotionally,
culturally, and socially in their individual, developmental histories. The terrain
on which each child's communicative and linguistic abilities developed is unique
in time and place. We can imagine that the setting of *First Grade Takes a Test* is
New York City: fictional 1st grader, George, one of the young "testees," may have
grown up in a middle-class family of European-American heritage, becoming a
speaker of a standard English by the age of 3 when he started preschool. Anna
Maria may have grown up in Manhattan where she became a speaker of African
American Language (AAL), a particular variant of English, by the age of 2; she
was, after all, precocious in many ways. Another 1st-grade child, unnamed in the
story, may have started to speak Russian in the country where he was born at the
age of one and a half but is now in the process of learning English as a second
language, becoming bilingual.

This diversity encompassing individual uniqueness persists in spite of schol-
arly assumptions about the universal wonders of language—that children "typically" learn it in particular sequences within defined periods of time (Brown,
1973; Pinker, 1994). Indeed, languages are wonderful because they are complex
human inventions, systems of symbols and meanings that groups of people have
used to communicate in particular terrains, often over long periods of time. But
human beings are equally wonderful because they differ and learn the ways of
communicating of those closest to them, at a tempo that suits each individual
learner.

Most languages are spoken and thus have interconnected systems, which
many think of as universal: of sound (phonology), grammar (syntax), lexicon
(semantics), and discourse (pragmatics). Of course there are languages that are
not spoken, such as American Sign Language (ASL), a language different from
English and used by some in the deaf community, and computer languages, in-

vented by humans to communicate with the machines so that these will—we hope—work on our behalf.

What matters for the purposes of this book is an appreciation of how numerous and varied languages are and how complex the connections are among the systems, how within "one language," such as English or Chinese, the systems vary significantly. Thus we more accurately refer to languages or the many dialects of English and Chinese.

In this first chapter we lay a foundation made up of people, languages, and classrooms in time and space, as we sketch the problematic terrain of current educational practices in the United States. We go on in Chapter 2 to processes of language learning and the impossibility of standardizing either language or children. The remaining chapters focus on "emergent bilinguals"; the importance of play and language, oral and written; the "basics" of writing; assessment of language and literacy; and the essences of teaching language and literacy in early childhood settings. These topics are linked by the diversity of young children in diverse times. Let's begin in the next section of this chapter by describing the great disconnect between the diversity of young learners and the homogeneous curricula created for them.

THE VERY PUZZLING DISCONNECT BETWEEN CLASSROOM CURRICULA AND DEMOGRAPHIC REALITY

The terrain of early childhood classrooms has been notably eroded by the cumulative pressures for accountability in education (National Commission on Excellence in Education, 1983; No Child Left Behind Act, 2001). As this book goes to press, the future of No Child Left Behind (NCLB) is uncertain; but its definition of *accountability* as mandated testing of students' academic achievement starting in 3rd grade is likely to remain. Although 3rd grade is at the upper boundary of *early childhood,* usually defined as birth through grade 2 or 3, many states have initiated tests for younger children as a way of preparing them for the rigors of the future or in order to receive federal funding for improving student achievement, especially in reading. (See Chapter 6 for more on this point.) Typically students in schools in need of funding do not pass the mandated tests and live in under-resourced neighborhoods where families have low incomes. Their children are labeled "at risk" and are often cast as deficient problems-to-be-fixed, especially in the areas of language and literacy.

Despite powerful legislation and mandates, we know from life experiences and research that children from *all* communities need and respond to a wide range of curricula and practices (Clay, 1998; Schweinhart & Weikart, 1997).

Children come from families or social groups that have their own rhythm, tempo, and volume level, their own amount of communication and interchange. Indeed, anyone with an awareness of recent economic and demographic changes in the United States (Cosentino de Cohen, Deterding, & Clewell, 2005) would declare the "norm" in sites like public schools to be diversity and difference, not homogeneity. Yet with a constricted focus on academic skills, those single-minded educators preoccupied with reading in English ignore the significant number of children in early education programs who are not English speakers (Garcia, 2005). Also ignored are children who are not "ready" for or are resistant to reading lessons because they have different interests or have disabilities.

So we state what is obvious to many: There is a very puzzling contrast—really an awesome disconnect—between the breathtaking diversity of schoolchildren and the uniformity, homogenization, and regimentation of classroom practices, from pre-kindergarten onward. To illustrate the disconnect, we next contrast the lifelike terrain of some classrooms for young children, with their calm, smooth spaces and action-filled bumpier spots, with the puzzling uniformity we see in curricula for language and literacy.

Diverse Activities at "Child Speed"

A calm, smooth place in a Head Start classroom for 3-year-olds, where one teacher and many of the children speak Spanish, might be the small area next to the book rack:

> Luisa is walking around, watching the other children, including Ana and Josué who are moving quickly to the *área de familia* (the family area). They take some plastic vegetables off a small cabinet and start playing with them. Luisa then takes a book from the rack and sits on a large pillow, still looking around the room and not at the book, which is upside down. An adult visitor in the room sits down next to her and starts talking to her in Spanish once Luisa has turned toward her. The adult is not quick to focus on the book.

Luisa is one of 16 children, mostly of Mexican heritage, who have selected an activity for "choice time," part of the HighScope curriculum (Hohmann, Banet, & Weikart, 1979) implemented by Head Start. What is striking about this period of time is that it is unstructured; it exemplifies a play-based curriculum. Indeed, to observers who are used to primary-grade classrooms, there is very little adult "intervention," except when activities show the bumpiness of too much exuberance or loud argument. No one is rushing to "read" with Luisa or to make sure she knows the book is upside-down, although eventually the adult sitting next to her turns it over and starts talking about it. In the meantime Luisa says not a word, but does make eye contact and nods her head a lot. Her home language, the teachers know, is neither Spanish nor English, but Mixteco, an indigenous Indian language of southern Mexico. In the next few months, Luisa will begin to learn Spanish as her second language. Her teachers allow her and her classmates the *time* to become learners of new languages. (For more of Luisa's story, see Chapter 3.)

"One-Size Fits All" at Adult Speed

Imagine how Luisa would respond (or not) in a classroom where there are no calm, smooth spaces available for sitting and watching or for slow conversation and where a primary goal is for children to learn the fundamentals of print. How could Luisa participate in this quick-paced lesson, scripted for teacher and learner, called "Say It Fast," with its dependence on knowledge of English and lack of connection to urban children's everyday activities:

1. Let's play say-it-fast. My turn: **lawn** (pause) **mower.** (Pause.) Say it fast. **Lawnmower.**
2. Your turn. Wait until I tell you to say it fast. **Lawn** (pause) **mower** (Pause.) Say it fast. (child says:) **"lawnmower."** (Repeat step 2 until firm.) (Engelmann, Haddox, & Bruner, 1983, p. 33)

These are the first two steps of a nine-step lesson, which includes instructions on how adults can correct children who don't "say it fast."

In contrast to our first example, this one can be described in terms of a particular learning objective (playing a word game as a warm-up to saying sounds), a teacher, and young learners who are to say particular things. Indeed, this so-called interaction is short and not very sweet and lacks any hint of diversity, for teacher and children are to follow a script, provided by the publisher, along with a teacher's guide that ensures specific "input" and specific "output." (Is this learning?) There is little distance between a lesson like this and an exchange between a ventriloquist and his doll-like dummy. Words are literally put in children's and teachers' mouths; the teacher fills the empty vessel of the child's mind. It's no surprise that these words seem disconnected from children's everyday language. And despite their unreal quality, lessons like this happen in thousands of homes and classrooms across the country, if one is to believe the marketing data for this best-selling curriculum.

A DIFFERENT SENSE OF TIME, A DIFFERENT USE OF SPACE

Sometimes teachers themselves may adopt different stances toward children's language and learning in different aspects of the curriculum. Mrs. Kay, for example, a 1st-grade teacher in a highly regulated (test-monitored) urban school, resisted being constrained by a curricular script. She allowed her children to spread themselves out, so to speak—to territorialize classroom space with their own affiliations, practices, and interests; and she also worked to get them in line with the uniform expectations for "1st graders"—soon to be test takers. Consider the following scenes, which present contrasting images of Mrs. Kay's language arts curriculum:

> Mrs. Kay has been modeling her own writing for her 1st graders. She knows that the after-school program is planning to take children to see the new Harry Potter movie. (The tickets will be provided, but not the snacks.) So, as her children sit on the classroom rug, Mrs. Kay writes about her own plans to "go out to eat" with her family and then "go to the movie." The children can write about their own plans for the movie, but they are not required to do so.
>
> When the children return to their worktables, they discuss their own Harry Potter plans (or non-plans). Lyron, who is always straightforward about money woes, explains that "I ain't going. I just went to see Scooby Doo and my dad rented (the old) Harry Potter."
>
> His peer Ezekial, also echoing a long-standing personal theme, explains that he isn't going either because "my grandma says Harry Potter is about witchcraft." Tionna is going but her plans are not about her family or, in fact, about watching the movie; they are about her friends and the popcorn she will buy with the money that will be in her pocket. When she starts writing, she produces:
>
>> Tomorrow me and Mandisa are going to see Harry Potter and we will sit biey (by) echuther (each other) and if she runots ut uv popckoer (runs out of popcorn) I will sher.

So Mrs. Kay modeled what seemed to her a relevant topic, but the children's responses indexed socioeconomic, cultural, and social relationships that differed from hers. Mrs. Kay, though, did not expect children to necessarily write about the topics she modeled, and generally the children did not. But Mrs. Kay did worry about the upcoming achievement tests and the expectations of the 2nd-grade teachers. And so she worried about the "basics" to be tested, including children's capitalization, punctuation, and "proper" usage.

Here is a sample of the grade-level expectations for usage, oral or written, given in the guidebook for Reading First teachers in the district:

Kindergarten Goals (Oral Language)

1. Use the correct form of irregular verbs, such as go (went), have (had, has), do (did). . . .
2. Use the correct article with a noun (a, an, the)
3. Speak in complete sentences.
4. Use verbs that agree with nouns (he doesn't). . . .
5. Use personal pronouns in compounds (Dad and I went to the park. . . .)

(Moats, 2004, p. 278)

First graders, then, should write with these constructions. Indeed, children "with language limitations" may need "direct teaching of sentence forms," including the explicit introduction of concepts like subject and predicate (Moats, 2004, p. 222).

But kindergartners, even if their home language is a variant of English, are not likely to speak in the prescribed formal ways. And, as 1st graders, Tionna, Lyron, and Ezekial all did not speak what would be regarded as a regional "standard" English. Moreover, each was still developing particular features of their home language—especially evident in overgeneralizations of rules, like "goodest," and inventions of possible words, like "borning" (always having been born or always alive). What would happen when, by midyear, children were urged to get in line, that is, to "say" what they wanted on paper . . . but in "proper" English? (More of this story appears in Chapter 2.)

Even in the same classroom, then, children might be allowed expressive space in one sense and constrained in another, particularly in those aspects of the curriculum that are formally tested. In so doing, the linguistic resources that ground their entry into literacy are transformed into problems, and the very communicative flexibility they might build is undermined as they are pressed to be ready for the test in a more urgent way than Cohen's fictional 1st graders.

CHILDHOODS IN CONTEMPORARY TIMES AND REGULATED SPACES

In our current slice of time, we see distressingly few classrooms and curricula that allow children either the time or space to learn about or through language in a way that they choose or that enables them to utilize what they already know. Unlike our fictional 1st graders, many children in contemporary centers and schools are pushed to become school learners instead of players, artists, talkers, loners, or friends with a diversity of backgrounds and interests. Thus most of their learning is configured step by step, according to yearlong periods of time, whether they are 2-year-olds in child care or 1st graders. At the end of each year, something happens—a metaphorical "step up" that can cause either delight or anxiety, including a transition to a new room, promotion to a new grade, or learning via more advanced materials. Increasingly these yearlong chunks of time have been marked by a singular event that causes much more anxiety than delight: a reading test. Thus, adults working in schools now feel pressed to look at children not as unique persons who follow their own interests and learn at their own tempo in diverse ways, but as young students who are becoming narrowly defined "readers."

The concept of childhood itself in the United States, then, has been transformed into a time period for particular kinds of learning, marked by rigid benchmarks or periodic endpoints—ends of school years, end-of-year tests, specific curricular content, like the alphabet and numbers. In other words, as Miriam Cohen suggests in *First Grade Takes a Test,* academic definitions of children's presents and futures have come to dominate the educational world. And in contrast to the era of developmentally appropriate practice (DAP, as described by Bredekamp & Copple, 1997, on behalf of the National Association for the Education of Young Children [NAEYC]), where appropriateness was defined by individual characteristics (e.g., a child's age or her abilities as perceived by teachers), today there are countless prescriptions for practice.

LOOKING AT DIFFERENCE
THROUGH A SOCIOCULTURAL LENS

Children with social and linguistic histories like Luisa's, Lyron's, and Tionna's could all be seen, side by side, as learners of language and literacy, once we change our theoretical lens. Instead of a narrow, behaviorist lens, we can choose one that is wide enough to encompass both diversity and complexity. In this section we introduce our theoretical perspective and will spin out its various aspects in the chapters that follow.

The key principle of our perspective: Regardless of children's culture, ethnicity, gender, language, race, or social class, their learning is profoundly social. It happens within relationships that some say begin between conception and birth—and others say begin at birth and so shape our experiences in and out of school. This idea underlies all that we present here and stems from the sociocultural theory of Vygotsky (1978) and others (Bruner & Haste, 1987; Rogoff, 2003), who portray human beings as people who both develop and learn. According to Vygotsky (1978), we learn everything twice (probably much more than twice, we think)—once on a social level with others and later within ourselves—intrapersonally or internally. Thus, a sociocultural theory does not ignore the internal or psychological, but the internal—what some call development—always links in complex ways to the external, the social and cultural.

In other words, according to this theory, learning is mediated by activities that are socially organized and often language based (Rogoff, 2003). Development and learning, then, are hard to envision without *language,* without *a system that allows for the representation of meaning.* Embedded within sociocultural theory for us is a sociolinguistic thread, in which we as users of language are put forward as social beings who experience and understand the world most often through language-mediated activities. Further, language is a cultural means of expression that, like culture itself, has multiple facets and uses. Thus, language is not an easily defined entity (such as the "English" in a dictionary or textbook for English learners); it varies much more than it stays the same—by person, neighborhood, region, country, and social situation (Cazden, 1970). In sum, the foundational sociolinguistic principle—that learning language, or as Halliday (1975) aptly put it, "learning how to mean"—is about learning what to say and how to say it across endlessly diverse situations. (The "saying," of course, could be verbal or nonverbal.)

So, too, with written language. In deciding "what they want to say" during writing time, or what texts themselves might say, children rely on familiar and typified voices (or social practices). From diverse experiences with print in families and communities, young children may accumulate idiosyncratic and varied bits of knowledge—letter forms, written names, perhaps a sense of how certain kinds of print sound when read. In response to literacy tasks in school, individual children rely on their own sense of what would sound "right" in the situation at hand; and that sense guides their efforts to appropriate, orchestrate, and adapt their diverse experiential and symbolic resources.

Moreover, "The point of entry and the path of progress may be different for any two children" (Clay, 1975, p. 7). Many researchers who have carefully observed young children engaged in literacy tasks "with scope" (i.e., reading or writing something beyond a letter or word; Clay, 1998, p. 238) do not find evidence for a set sequence of developmental learning beginning with letters and sounds. Rather, they find that these aspects of written language are a part of young learners' messy mix of knowledge and know-how (Chittenden & Salinger, with Bussis, 2001; Clay, 1975, 1977; Dyson, 1987, 1989, 1999; Glupczynski, 2007; Heath, 1983). In Clay's (1975) words:

> A simplification achieved by dealing firstly with letters, then words, and finally word groups (and text types) may be easy for teachers (researchers, educational program developers, and test makers) to understand but children learn on all levels at once. (p. 19)

THE NORM IS DIVERSITY

In the early 21st century we seem stuck in a time warp in which children who embody certain kinds of diversity have become the problem, and standardization has become the "fix," though not a quick or workable one. You might think that the way to fix the "problem" of breathtakingly diverse schoolchildren who may or may not meet standards is to connect them with diverse curricula. However, as we've said, the opposite has happened.

Those who have recently set policy related to language and literacy insist that children and teachers in schools and centers live with a disconnect, with this educational paradox: There is a profusion of human diversity in our schools and an astonishingly narrow offering of curricula. Indeed, they are recycling the view of children as empty vessels to be filled by behaviorist-oriented, scripted lessons. In light of this paradox, we say flatly that something is terribly wrong.

It is wrong because the shifts in policy, which have led to constraining curricula, need revision and reenvisioning that take into account child learners' individual histories and what they are *able* to do in and out of the classroom. Narrow visions need to be replaced with complex scenes that are spacious enough for children's diverse ways of being, within a time frame and on curricular terrain that expands way beyond adult prescriptions. That more welcoming terrain has space for the strengths and resources of children who are "different"—that is, children who might be

- Resistant to structured lessons
- Physically but not linguistically gifted
- Other than middle class or white
- Able to become bilingual or multilingual over time
- Boys that choose to wear skirts in the dress-up area, or girls who refuse to wear skirts ever
- More interested in gerbils than letters of the alphabet
- Mastering a "nonstandard" dialect of English by the age of 3
- Behaving more like an artist or expert player than a reader
- And so on

These children are condemned to be invisible within the scope of an extremely narrow curricular lens.

In short, we are proclaiming the good news that difference and diversity are the new "normal." Our vision is not children who speak English only or read or pass tests at the earliest moment. Rather, our general goal is early education that makes sense to children and their teachers. More specifically our goal is the sociolinguistic flexibility that opens children up to school learning and to life experiences unbounded by scripts and test scores. With this goal of flexibility in mind, we turn in Chapter 2 to ways in which young children learn language unbounded by narrow standards.

2. Standardized Language, Standardized Childhood

Lyron, African American, and Ezekial, Mexican American, are two 6-year-old "dudes" making "tight" cars out of Legos. Those cars are used to do battle with another Lego player, Brad. Lyron helps Ezekial make a big car.

> *Ezekial:* Hey, this is going to be tight! Put that on. This is going to be the goodest—
> *Lyron:* the *baddest* car
> *Ezekial:* Because look, because we're going to destroy again. . . .
>   We got a *mean* car. Mrs. Kay! Look at me and Lyron's car!
> *Mrs. Kay:* Wow! That is so cool. Wow, you guys!
> *Ezekial:* We got the *meanest* car.

(See Figure 2.1 for transcript conventions.)

Lyron and Ezekial are busy regulating, negotiating, and expressing their relationship with each other. In this car-making event, Lyron is playing out the identity of a tough "dude" (his word). He corrects Ezekial, not because he has overgeneralized an inflectional morpheme (i.e., the superlative suffix "est"), but because Ezekial has not used an appropriate "dude" word for their battle-ready car: that car is "so good" that it's "bad" (Smitherman, 1994, p. 52, on African American Language [AAL]). Ezekial tries to get on Lyron's communicative wavelength with "meanest"; his "mean," though, seems based on the car's function as a "destroy[er]," not on its superb quality.

Lyron and Ezekial demonstrate that learning language is inextricably linked to learning to be with others in a socially complex world. Key to that learning is the human capacity to appropriate and adapt language to the communicative circumstance. Indeed, their language standards—their judgments about whether expectations had been met for appropriate language use—were tied to identity and to the situation at hand.

FIGURE 2.1. Conventions Used in the Presentation of Transcripts.

(abc) Parentheses enclosing text contain notes, usually about contextual and nonverbal information (e.g., moves hands to scare children).

(abc) Brackets contain explanatory information inserted into quotations by us, rather than by the speaker.

A-B-C Capitalized letters separated by hyphens indicate that letters were spoken or words were spelled aloud by the speaker.

ABC A capitalized word or phrase indicates increased volume.

abc An italicized word indicates a stressed word or words in Spanish, which are followed by English translations in parentheses.

// Double slashed lines inserted into a speaking turn indicates a rhythmic break, for example,
    All girls: Boom chicka// my ha::ir

/ A single slashed line inserted into a line of written text indicates that an additional line break was present in the original, for example,
    I get tier of that/calling me mame (ma'am) So I will call
       her mame. . . .

/a:/ A colon inserted into word or sentence indicates that the sound of the previous letter was elongated

. . . Ellipsis points indicate omitted data; when they are inserted in the beginning of a line, they indicate omitted speaking turn(s), e.g.,
    Tommy: No, not me. He, Stoo:ky!
    . . .
    How you do that, Stooky-hole?
    Ashley: Stooky-hole? How you say that?

( ) Empty parentheses indicate an unclear utterance.

Note: Conventional punctuation marks are used to indicate ends of utterances or sentence, usually indicated by slight pauses on the audiotape. Commas refer to pauses within words or word phrases.

This stance toward standards is strikingly different from that undergirding efforts to regulate schooling for young children. Those efforts assume language is homogenous and hierarchical; that is, quite apart from any particular context, there is a "best" way to speak and to write. Against the backdrop of such a standard, the most pressing curricular issues have been focused on the "different" child, including the speaker of a "nonstandardized" English and the one just learning English in school.

Sociolinguists make a distinction between a "standard" language and the historical, political, and ideological process of "standardization" (e.g., Wolfram, Adger, & Christian, 1999). Through this process, institutions like schools work to suppress the inherent variability of language by authorizing uniformity. Yet given that the majority of children in our urban public schools are not white or middle class in background, is it sensible to base curricula on a vision of *the* normative child? Would abandoning that norm and acknowledging the normalcy of difference threaten standards in our schools? Would it, and how would it, influence our teaching goals and strategies? These are the central concerns of this chapter and, more broadly, this book.

Taking a cue from Cohen's teacher in *First Grade Takes a Test,* we first describe children's tremendous language-learning capacities. We frame our evolving description with different views of child language learning. Each view has highlighted different aspects of what language learners can do. Second, we consider how these varied views may contribute to a rethinking of the "normal" child learner; to do so, we foreground children who speak a nonstandardized English. Our goal is to explore what it would mean to embrace the normalcy of difference.

THEORIES OF LANGUAGE LEARNING

Tracy and Berry were student observers in Mrs. Kay's class once a week. They and their peers talked with Anne about language learning in that class:

> *Tracy:* Our teacher (Mrs. Kay) reads these books called *Junie B Jones* (Park, 1992–2005)? Have you heard of that? And in the books, the author has written her up to speak like what she thinks a 5-year-old would speak like and um the little girl—"I runned across the field and I sawed my friend." . . . And the children mimic that in the first grade, and it's wrong. They were doing this exercise where they correct grammar. And one child said something and it was wrong, and it was incorrect. And another student yelled out, "AAh ha he gotted it wrong." Well, you know, there's the pot calling the kettle black. And I don't know if those books are the best thing to be reading them when they're learning English.
> *Berry:* . . . We were taught standard English grammar. If you don't say it this way, you were wrong. . . .

In this conversation, Tracy puts forward her belief that children learn language through "mimicking"—that is, through imitation. Moreover, she and Berry both imply that correction is a useful strategy for "teaching" young children language.

As we suggested in Chapter 1, these views of learning, emphasizing imitation and correction, inform curricular scripts being enacted widely in early childhood classrooms. And yet scholars of child language have long since dismissed these behaviorist views (Skinner, 1957) in favor of those that better account for children's complex language learning. Below we turn to the first of these views, developed by psycholinguists who were inspired by the highly influential linguist Noam Chomsky.

Language Learning as Web-Spinning: A Focus on Child Grammar

For N. Chomsky (1968), any theory of child language has to account for children's acquisition of grammar. By "grammar," Chomsky does not mean the knowledge of what is regarded as "correct" usage in school, which is how Tracy and Berry would define it. Rather, he means the knowledge of how sounds and words are combined to form meaningful utterances in whatever language variant one speaks (whether "standard" or not). Long before children confront explicit instruction on parts of speech or "correct" sentences, they know how to produce meanings through the arrangement of words and sounds in systematic, highly complex ways. Their speech (linguistic performance) suggests an underlying, albeit unconscious, linguistic competence. Indeed, the cognitive scientist Steven Pinker (1994) describes language as a human instinct, more akin to a spider's web spinning than to conscious learning.

During the 1960s and 1970s, many linguists and psycholinguists were inspired by Noam Chomsky's (1965) notion of a Language Acquisition Device— an inborn ability to figure out complex grammatical rules. They followed small, primarily middle-class children around their homes, aiming to understand the evolving grammar of their early utterances (e.g., Brown, 1973). They taped children's utterances and transcribed them; then they coded their early two-word utterances for the basic meanings they conveyed, meanings like *agent, action,* or *object.* In this way they could examine how children arranged those basic meanings; in other words, they studied early syntax.

For example, at around 18 months or 2 years, English-speaking children produce utterances like "Allgone bubbles," expressing nonexistence, a common basic meaning. "No nap" expresses another common idea, negation. "Baby eat" or "Mommy eat" convey an agent and an action. However "Eat Mommy" or "Eat baby" would not occur, because this arrangement of agent and action does not occur in English syntax. Thus, young children produce utterances that they have never heard; they do not simply mimic the speech around them. At the same time, their utterances suggest that they are deducing rules about how meanings are arranged.

Over time, children's utterances get longer as more meaning units (i.e., more morphemes) are expressed in one utterance. Thus, researchers have been able to construct predictable plots about how children's language changes over time—plots about, for example, children progressing from "no treat" to "I no want treat," then "I not want treat," and, finally, the nicely formed but equally firm, "I don't want it" (Klima & Bellugi-Klima, 1966).

In this developmental story of language learning, the star is a child who functions as a little linguist; that child linguist is attuned to salient parts of the language and how those parts are arranged (i.e., to grammar). The child begins by expressing underlying meanings with one-word and then two-word utterances, gradually differentiating a more powerful grammar for expressing increasingly (infinitely) complex utterances.

Consider, for example, the following interaction among a teacher and 4-year-olds at a public pre-kindergarten in New York City, serving mainly Cantonese-speaking families (Genishi, Yung-Chan, & Stires, 2000). In this example (not previously published), Alice, Andy, and Kenneth are entranced by the process by which a caterpillar undergoes metamorphosis and becomes a butterfly. Their teacher Ms. Yung is reading from *See How They Grow: Butterfly* (Ling, 1992) and showing the class a picture of the caterpillar:

> *Ms. Yung:* It looks like this now, you see? Okay, we don't scare the caterpillar, okay? (referring to the caterpillar that the class is observing at other times of the day in a "butterfly box")
> *Kenneth:* He, he eat you!
> *Ms. Yung:* They won't eat you. How would you like it if they did this to you all the time? (moves hands to "scare" children) We don't want to bother the caterpillar, okay?
> *Andy:* (some Cantonese first) Gonna turn butterfly!
> *Ms. Yung:* Yes, it's going to turn into a butterfly.
> *Kenneth:* You, you, you gonna open it, gonna open and let the butterfly, school, out and fly!
> *Ms. Yung:* Yeah, we are going to let the butterfly out.
> *Andy:* (some Cantonese first) Butterfly! Big butterfly!
> *Ms. Yung:* (continues reading about the caterpillar growing bigger and bigger)
> *Alice:* Ms. Yung. (motioning with her hands to show something small) Small, still small. Baby!

In the above excerpt, "the child" is visibly spinning the intricate patterns of language, but because the children are becoming bilingual in Cantonese and English, their word combinations sometimes are two-word combinations of meanings (e.g., "big butterfly" [Brown, 1973]), enhanced with motions and gestures, and at other times elaborate combinations that convey complicated ideas (e.g., "Gonna turn butterfly" or "you gonna open it . . ."). Kenneth can say the compound noun *butterfly* and also use the verb *fly* in an appropriate way. Moreover, Kenneth audibly grapples with the challenges of creating a complex sentence ("gonna open and let the butterfly, school, out and fly!") while trying to embed the skeleton of an adverbial phrase (something like "out of the school"). Adding to the complexity is the children's knowledge of their first language, Cantonese, which allows pronoun omission in the subject position and does not use definite or indefinite articles (i.e., "the" and "a").

These 4-year-olds would not be expected to explain parts of speech ("butterfly" as a compound noun), inflectional morphemes ("ing"), much less to discuss what syntactic rules are violated when someone says "gonna turn butterfly." Thus, the children's everyday talk with their teacher illustrates the main point of the developmental psycholinguists of the 1960s and 1970s: the complexity of grammatical formations is far too sophisticated to be deliberately taught. The very idea of trying to teach these notions to a young child is absurd. Rather, the conceptual tools of this definition of language allow us to appreciate the pattern-detecting intelligence behind children's errors (e.g., their overregularization of inflectional endings, like past tense, as in "goed," plurals, as in "footses," or comparatives like "goodest").

Given all this child-language skill at which to marvel, Why, one might ask, are concerns about children's language at the heart of intense educational discussions? These concerns, though, are not about language as an abstract rule system or an evolutionary gift. They are about language as used by particular children—about speech; and they are focused on aspects of speech that are viewed as indicators of social difference and academic risk. To move closer to these concerns, we consider next the view of children's language learning we emphasize, one in which language is learned through children's social participation in everyday worlds.

Language Learning as Interacting:
A Focus on Children's Sociocultural Worlds

For Katherine Nelson (1996, 2007), language is not like web-spinning, although she, too, acknowledges its biological base. Like others influenced by the Russian psychologist Vygotsky (1978, 1987), she emphasizes that a *biological* capacity has enabled humans to develop symbol systems; those systems, organized and used in social activities, are *cultural* capacities. Language—the central symbolic and cultural tool of human societies—enables people to connect with others, to represent and communicate about experiences, and in the process, to declare their own identities as participants in their worlds (Lindfors, 1999).

Although elders do not teach children grammar, they do guide children's engagement in the activities that form the rhythms of daily experiences, activities like waking, bathing, getting dressed, eating. Through participation in these activities, children acquire social as well as linguistic knowledge (Bruner, 1983; Ochs & Schieffelin, 2001). They learn to focus on others, to infer the relevance and meaning of their actions, to anticipate those actions, to act contingently themselves, and thereby to take coordinated turns—all acts that are essential for nonverbal and verbal communication.

Consider, for example, the way in which Amy, just 21 months old, engages in a complex interaction with her mother Marlene about a baby doll, an important cultural object. In the following vignette, from Miller's (1982, p. 113) study of three working-class European-American children, Marlene teases Amy, and in her response, Amy reveals that she understands that her mother is teasing, and moreover, that she also understands how caregivers act toward crying babies:

> Amy is sitting next to her mother Marlene. She covers her doll with a blanket.
>
> > *Mother:* Throw that baby on the floor. (Marlene's tone is stern, mildly threatening.)
> > *Amy: No*-oh. (Amy arranges doll in lap, settling herself in chair.)
> > *Marlene:* Why?
> > *Amy:* Cause.
> > *Marlene:* Make the baby cry? (Marlene's tone is sympathetic, especially on "cry.")
> > *Amy: No*-oh. (Amy looks at doll. (She apparently misunderstands Marlene's tone.)) Baby. There, baby. (Amy lifts up corner of blanket, looks at Marlene. Amy pats doll.)
> > *Marlene:* Baby goin to sleep?
> > *Amy:* No sleep. (Amy shakes head.) Ah. (Amy pats doll. Amy picks up doll.) Here Mommy. Here. (Amy places doll on Marlene's lap.)
> > *Marlene:* Thank you.
> > *Amy:* Baby here. (Marlene wraps blanket around doll.) Going to sleep. (Marlene holds doll against shoulder, patting it.)

Amy speaks primarily in two-word sentences, but, with Marlene's help, she participates in a complex event. In her role as caregiver, she would not—and she knows her mother would not—throw the baby on the floor. "There baby," she says, as Marlene no doubt said to her. Amy thus illustrates how children appropriate words from familiar events. They use others' words to take their own action—to make requests and demands, to express their feelings, to comfort and to comment, and in other functional ways, learn "how to mean" (Halliday, 1975).

Through such interactive experiences, children develop both linguistic knowledge and, more broadly, social knowledge of how language is used in particular social situations. Sociolinguists refer to this dual knowledge as communicative competence (Hymes, 1972). Amy, for example, understood that mothers express concern about crying babies and that they do so through comforting nonverbal and verbal actions, like patting the baby and saying, "There, baby." She was also learning that expected behavior can be violated in another kind of event, one that could be called "teasing."

Teasing events were important to Marlene, a way in which she socialized her daughter to stand up for herself in what could be a tough world (Miller, 1996). But parent-child teasing events are differentially common in our society. Some readers may smile with recognition at this event, and others may be taken aback by a mother's tough talk. Amy's event thus illustrates how a sociocultural view of language learning turns attention from language as a human universal to language as a mediator of human diversity.

All children learn language, but their learning is cultural and shaped by the socioeconomic, linguistic, and political circumstances in which their lives take shape. Children learn, for example, varying ways of telling stories, of praying, of asking questions and showing deference—and even of deciding who is an authority figure (e.g., Erickson, 2007; Heath, 1983; Levinson, 2007; Philips, 1972). Their language in use thus echoes with the human relationships and daily experiences that give their lives meaning. In this approach, then, children are not so much little linguists as emergent social beings, adapting to, and participating in, their cultural worlds.

Adults, including teachers, have a much clearer role in children's language learning in this sociocultural view than in a psycholinguistic one. Teachers, like caregivers, organize their day with recurrent, interactive events, like morning routines, story time, and sharing. Within the structure of those familiar events, children are provided with things to talk about and people with whom to talk. Adults offer guidance of various kinds (arranging the environment, modeling how to interact with objects and other people, guiding children's efforts, providing needed information). Ideally, they also try to tap children's eye view, noticing what children judge as relevant and meaningful and, through interaction, deepening and broadening their understandings.

Unlike caregivers, teachers have particular responsibilities for children's academic learning in mathematics, literacy, science, and social studies. Still, as Nelson (1996) explains, children's resources for this learning are rooted in their everyday experiences and in their stories of those experiences. Implicit in tales of what "we do" and "I did" are discourses of "time, space, geography, religion, gender roles, biology, and the natural world" (p. 218). In school, then, teachers may help children draw on their implicit knowledge and formalize it, by talking about their experiences—recontextualizing them—within broader disciplinary frames of reference.

For example, an array of kinds of implicit knowledge and know-how is evident in Alice, Andy, and Kenneth's participation with Ms. Yung in the informal science lesson. Collectively, they reference the passage of time, notions of growth and transformation, and even confined and open space. They "get" metamorphosis—soon the caterpillar will become a "big butterfly" that will seek a space larger than a preschool classroom. For now, though, it is "still small," a kind of "baby," as Alice points out.

Moreover, the children articulate these conceptual understandings at the same time that they manage local expectations for communication. As alert social beings, they carefully coordinate their turns with Ms. Yung's, building on her and each other's utterances to sustain the topic. Note, for instance, how Ms. Yung repeats and expands Andy's comment on the future of the caterpillar and then Kenneth builds yet further; he talks about the freeing of the butterfly, as it were, when its time has come. That time, notes Andy, will be when it's "big," but not now, to return to Alice's point. Together, teacher and children enact a shared social world in which familiar vocabulary and syntax are stretched as new ideas are grappled with.

From this perspective on language, educators may observe more dimensions of children's language learning—its interactional intricacy, its functional possibilities, and situational variation. Moreover, this perspective suggests the importance of educators' learning about each child as a person whose social sense and knowledge resources come from a diversity of involvements as a friend, a family member, and a participant in community and popular cultures. In this way, they are more likely to understand and build on children's meanings (Gonzalez, Moll, & Amanti, 2005; Vasquez, Pease-Alvarez, & Shannon, 1994).

Educators' efforts, though, are supported and constrained by the districts, communities, and society in which they work. This brings us to the final perspective on language learning we share here. This *dialogic* perspective alerts us to language as not only deeply *personal,* tied to our identities as family and community members, but also as *political.* That is, ways of using language are interconnected with complex social dialogues about appropriate, "proper," and intelligent behavior. These notions are on display in new expectations about child language, the kind that drives some of that test-taking going on in early childhood classrooms.

Language Learning and Ideology:
A Focus on Societal Dialogues About Language

For the Russian philosopher Bakhtin (1981), language is a social phenomenon that exists as it is used by people to address one another; that is, it exists in dialogue.

Moreover, these speakers exist in a complex world of differences, even if they share a common language like English. Among such differences are those related to age, gender, ethnic cultures, social classes, occupations, and academic disciplines. Children, then, become language users by drawing on the voices—the social registers (like "cool dude" talk), the regional and ethnic dialects—that surround them.

Children, like those populating this chapter, are socialized into language use in different families, with different socioeconomic resources and challenges, in different regions of the country, with different sociocultural histories. For example, Mrs. Kay and her children spoke varied dialects of English. Dialects are systematic variations in a language's grammatical rules, associated with geographic, social, and cultural boundaries. These variations are audible in the ways speech sounds are combined and pronounced (phonology), the ways words are combined to form grammatical sentences (syntax), the meanings of words (semantics), and the way speech varies among situations (pragmatics). The dialects considered "standard" are those spoken by the most powerful people in a certain geographic area, but they are no more systematic than the dialects labeled "nonstandard."

This normal variation becomes a problem in schools, which are typically adapted to the dominant social system and stress standardized knowledge (Cohen, 1971/2000). Children who vary from what is considered the "norm" in language use—from that of the dominant societal group—may be viewed as having problems that need to be fixed, not as potentially adroit speakers with the capacity to adapt to new situations.

Similarly, there is wide variation in the normal rate of vocabulary learning among very young children. As Nelson (2007) explains, children may gain a repertoire of 50 words at 13 months or 25 months; that rate does not index child intelligence but, rather, individual disposition, family styles of interaction, and cultural ways with words. In school, language use may be reduced to vocabulary and that vocabulary may be regarded as an index of socioeconomic status and academic potential (Hart & Risley, 1995). But all children have, and can continue to learn, ways of naming their worlds, given curricular opportunities to build on what they know (Delpit, 2003). There is no need to assume that a child's vocabulary learning must be "fixed"; it must be engaged.

In brief, given a dialogic view of language, entering into language use is also entering into societal dialogues; in those dialogues, a child's words may carry unanticipated reverberations for certain listeners, echoes of social places and attitudes. This adds elements of critical reflectiveness to teachers' work (Godley, Sweetland, Wheeler, Minnici, & Carpenter, 2006; Ladson-Billings, 2001; Nieto, 2002; Samway, 2006).

That work includes monitoring one's own evaluative judgments about individual interest and ability. Teachers need patience, trust, and skill to interact with children, especially those whose ways with words are different from their own "normal" ways. These qualities also support teachers' efforts to more fully know children as communicators by observing them in different settings and activities, with different interactional partners, focusing on different topics, and using different symbolic tools, including languages. Moreover, teachers need commitment and flexibility to make connections with families across boundaries of language, not to mention those of geographic space and time (given work and child-care schedules and differential access to transportation).

Children themselves may also notice and react to language differences. Thus, teachers' responsibilities include providing children with models, guidance, and opportunities to talk about and act amid social and cultural language differences (Derman-Sparks, 1989; *Rethinking Schools* [a magazine devoted to critical school reform and practice]). Ultimately, the educational goal is to help children adapt to, participate in, and negotiate a range of communicative situations in our sociolinguistically complex world.

To dramatize the interplay between what is assumed to be "normal" and the normal differences in schools, we take as a kind of object lesson young children's use of a particular variant of English, referred to herein as African American Language (AAL). We consider how each discussed conception of language and language learning contributes to our understanding of this phenomenon and, also, of the teaching goals and strategies within which it matters.

STANDARDIZING CHILDREN AND LANGUAGE: THE CASE OF AAL

The trend toward more structured early childhood programs is sometimes accompanied by language arts standards that seem surprisingly outdated; that is, they seem based on the notion of rote learning, which predates the last 50 years of research (Skinner, 1957). Readers may recall, for example, the language goals for K–1 *Reading First* teachers in Mrs. Kay's district (see Chapter 1). Or, as a further illustration, consider the following excerpts from the California State Department of Education curricular guidelines for kindergartners:

> For some (children), instruction begins first with statement repetition and progresses to statement production. Instruction in this focus area . . . (must include):
>
> 1. Explicit modeling of standard English
> 2. Carefully constructed linguistic units that progress from short sentences to longer sentences
> 3. Frequent opportunity to repeat sentences

4. Additional, gentle modeling emphasizing specific elements of sentences that are omitted or pronounced incorrectly
5. Strategically designed instruction that shifts from statement repetition to statement production
6. Structured statement production whereby students first generate responses to questions from pictures or prompts and then generate questions or responses without prompts (California State Department of Education, 2007, p. 39)

The 1st-grade guidelines are similar, emphasizing modeling and repetition, although they are more focused on specific conventions, as the following instructional guidelines indicate (from p. 59):

3. Carefully selecting, sequencing, and scheduling instructional targets that allow learners to master one form (e.g., my) before progressing to the next (e.g., his/her or your/yours)
4. Providing frequent opportunities to repeat sentences
5. Strategically integrating instruction requiring students to discern the correct usage (his/hers, your/yours)

Such recommended strategies include no apparent recognition of children as web spinners, who actively detect language patterns and whose progress may be manifested as errors (e.g., overgeneralized rules). The strategies also make no clear provisions for children as social negotiators, who use language to build social worlds with others. Moreover, the strategies include no direct acknowledgment of the many varieties and variations of language spoken by children, although such variation is the norm "everywhere" (Bailey, 2004, p. 6).

Thus, the official guidance is of limited use in understanding how to make sense of and respond to children's speech. Consider, for example, the following scene:

A small group of East San Francisco Bay 1st graders is discussing the relative size of varied creatures and objects—including God. Among the children are Jameel and Monique, both African American, and Berto, who is Latino. Following is a small excerpt from their talk.

Jameel: But what about God. He's bigger than everything.
Berto: No he isn't. (And then more loudly.) He AIN'T BIGGER THAN EVERYTHING.
Monique: You don't know.
. . .
Berto: He's not bigger than Jesus.
Jameel: Jesus his son.
Berto: His baby.

Jameel: Son.
Berto: Baby.
Jameel: Son.

. . .

Berto: Daughter!
Monique: Son. Son. He really son. Uh-huh. He's the son.
He *is.*

These children, all students of teacher Louise Rosenkrantz, were skillful language users, vigorous discussants, successful literacy learners—and speakers of "nonstandard" varieties of English (data from project reported in full in Dyson, 1993). For example, Jameel and Monique, as speakers of AAL, share syntactic or word-arrangement options that allow them to "correctly" use forms of what linguists call the copula *to be,* as in "He really son." In other words, they are able to delete, rather than only contract, forms of *to be* (Rickford, 1999; Smitherman, 1977, 1994). Most strikingly, in the last line of the transcript, Monique moves from calmly pointing out that "he really son" to more pointedly and urgently saying "He's the son. He *is.*"

The children's use of patterned options evidences their developing control of AAL. That language itself is a testament to the language-generating power of human beings, given its roots in the intermingling of languages during slavery. Ripped from their home countries, isolated from other slaves who spoke their mother tongues, denied instruction in language and literacy, still, Africans used humanity's linguistic powers in those inhumane conditions to adapt, synthesize, and stretch old ways with words to new ways that evolved over the generations (Rickford, 1999).

Clearly, becoming skillful language users involves more than linearly progressing along a route to language correctness. It involves a broadening interactional responsiveness and flexibility. In the following sections, we use each discussed conception of language learning as a framework for considering aspects of language learning and teaching that would allow all children linguistic respect as well as access to the Language of Wider Communication (LWC)—that is, standardized English. We feature in our discussion children from varied urban classrooms, especially Mrs. Kay's student Tionna, a speaker of African American Language and a child with a propensity for oral and written storytelling.

Spinning (Devalued) Webs

In his web-spinning conception of language learning, Pinker (1994) dismisses the sort of variations codified as "dialect differences" as "trifling" (p. 28).

He emphasizes the sophisticated grammatical rule-construction that undergirds all human language use. As documented by sociolinguists (e.g., Labov, 1972; Smitherman, 1977), African American Language, like all dialects, including those judged "standard," is just "language," just systematic, rule-governed, sound- (or gesture-) symbol connections.

Considering children's language use from this perspective is useful. It alerts us to the *different linguistic rules* children may be learning; this is especially important for children beyond the earliest levels of language learning (i.e., roughly, those 3 and older [Seymour & Roeper, 1999]). For example, when AAL speakers construct an utterance like "Jesus his son," their speech evidences a linguistic difference—one evident in adult speech in their families. If 21-month-old Amy had spoken an utterance in which the copula was deleted (e.g., like "Baby crying"), that would not evidence a linguistic difference characteristic of her community but a strictly developmental one; that is, Amy's talk would not be reflecting a linguistic feature of her family. However, if Kenneth, a Cantonese speaker, had said "Baby crying," we would not be sure whether this was a developmental characteristic of Kenneth's English or one related to the nature of Cantonese grammar—or both. Judgments about "correct" or "appropriate" language are complex, a theme we will return to in Chapter 6.

Moreover, as the web-spinning view accurately highlights, young children cannot be explicitly taught their developing grammatical system. In school settings, though, children's linguistic rule system may indeed be viewed as just "wrong." This has potential consequences for both oral and written language development. For example, in order to figure out the nature of the written symbol system, children must rely on their speech. They listen to what sounds right as they construct and monitor their own efforts to write and to read. And yet, what sounds "right" to young children will vary, at least in part, for developmental and sociocultural reasons. For this reason, a devaluing of children's vernacular may interfere with their reliance on their own language sense (i.e., with their metalinguistic reasoning about how speech and text relate).

For example, in Mrs. Kay's class, children like Tionna and her peers Janette and Ebony—the most consistent speakers of AAL—did not respond well to explicit correction in and of itself. Rather, they responded to Mrs. Kay's efforts to fix their written vernacular with silence. They seemed to know that, eventually, their teacher, as judge and chief language fixer, would do just that (full project reported in Dyson, 2006). An illustration of this is provided by the following vignette (analyzed fully in Dyson, 2008a):

> Tionna and her table mates have been heavily into Christmas on this December Day. Amidst the claims and counterclaims about big trees

and big presents, Tionna claims that she has the biggest present of all. Listening to her own voice, she then writes "it's big" like this: *is big.* (*It's* is pronounced "i's" in African American Language due to phonological rules. As Geneva Smitherman (personal communication, June 6, 2004) explained: "In 'it's' the *t* may be deleted and the resulting pronunciation of *s* mirrors or retains the voicelessness of the *t*"; that is, the vocal chords do not vibrate when one says the sound of *t* or *s*, unlike when one makes the sound of *d* or *z*).

Mrs. Kay has been circulating among the children, and she stops to read Tionna's page (see Figure 2.2).

> *Mrs. Kay:* Does that make sense, "I got it from my mommy and is big"? (Mrs. Kay is not saying what Tionna said. Tionna said /i's/; Mrs. Kay is saying /iz/.)

Tionna does not respond, and so Mrs. Kay returns to Tionna's text, pointing to the *and.*

> *Mrs. Kay:* "a::nd" (hopeful pause)

Tionna still does not respond.

> *Mrs. Kay:* What word could you be missing?
> *Tionna:* "the"
> *Mrs. Kay:* "It."
> *Tionna:* (reading) "and it's"

Tionna then adds an editorial caret and writes *it;* the text now reads *and it is big.*

> *Mrs. Kay:* Good for you!

Using her speech as a major resource, Tionna presented a problem to Mrs. Kay. Mrs. Kay thought Tionna's text had a grammatical problem—a missing word. If Tionna was having a problem, though, it was spelling a contraction, not missing a word. In fact, the very next day, Tionna again spelled the contraction "*it's*" as *I-S.*

Tionna had various such "problems"—*me*'s that should be *I*'s (e.g., "Me and Janette like him"), *and*'s that shouldn't exist at all or perhaps should be commas instead (e.g., "make up and a Barbie house and some ice cream and pizza and . . ."), not to forget the whole issue of *be*'s that should be *is*'s or *are*'s (e.g., "If you be bad . . ."). But Tionna *was* learning to write without mastering these so-called basics . . . which made them seem not so basic for a young child who is beginning to write.

FIGURE 2.2. Tionna's Big Present.

Moreover, there was no official attention to variations in how people speak or write, no discourse or way of talking about talk that Tionna and her teacher could have appropriated. And yet it may be at just such moments of heightened attention—when *i's*, for example, might be rendered as *it's*—that young children are most receptive to deliberate attention to language differences (i.e., to the metalinguistic work such attention entails).

To illustrate, in her classic study, Piestrup (1973) focused on reading instruction for AAL-speaking 1st graders in 14 classrooms in the San Francisco Bay area.

She documented the child confusion that could result if teachers continuously interrupted children as they read, attempting to teach "pronunciation" instead of "reading" (the ability to make sense of written codes [see also Delpit, 1998, and Meier, 2008]). This "instructional" strategy may teach children not to trust their own good language sense.

For example, in the following dialogue from Piestrup's data (1973, pp. 54–55), a teacher (T) inadvertently leads a child (C1) away from a correct reading of a text and into peer silliness; she does this by interrupting his reading with a pronunciation lesson on the interdental form of /th/, which is pronounced /d/ in AAL. (Bracketed contextual information inserted into Piestrup's transcript for clarity.)

> C1: (reading *they* in his text) "Dey—"
> T: Get your finger out of your mouth.
> C1: (continuing reading) "call—"
> T: Start again.
> C1: "Dey call," What i' it? What is it?
> T: What's this word?
> C2: "Dey."
> C1: (who must assume the word is not *they,* since that's what he read
>   when the teacher first intervened) "Dat."
> C2: "Dat."
> C3: "Dey."
> C4: (laughs)

In Piestrup's study, effective reading teachers did not interrupt when the children were reading and, moreover, found ways to build on children's lively playfulness. They initiated many group conversations about text meaning in which children listened and responded to one another as well as to their teacher. However, the most effective teachers *did* attend straightforwardly to dialect differences that influenced meaning and spelling, as when, for example, a group of children confused *feet* and *feed* (pronounced similarly, since the final consonant [/d/] was reduced; that is, it lost its vocal chord vibration and became [/t/]). Here was a clear occasion for calling attention to differences in how words are pronounced and for emphasizing the ending sounds of words.

If teacher attention is going to be paid when children are confused, and if children are not going to be confused by their teacher's attention, educators must be linguistically informed about the home languages, including the English variants, spoken by their children, and to do that best, they need to listen to and interact with children's parents and communities.

Still, other than being aware and respectful of children's linguistic knowledge, so as not to do damage, the web-spinning theory leaves significant aspects of language learning and teaching unaddressed. In the next section, we broaden our focus on children's language to include social participation and communicative flexibility in school.

Constructing Social World(s)

Jameel, Monique, and Berto, who intensely discussed the relative sizes of God and Jesus, were clearly skilled conversationalists. They were building on one another's sentences syntactically (e.g., by repeating and varying sentence structures "Jesus his son" "His baby.") and, also, semantically (e.g., by linking key phrases and words, like "God," "Jesus," "son," and "daughter"). Monique's varied ways of using the copula suggested that she could use different grammatical options for rhetorical purposes, like emphasis ("He really son. Uh-huh. He's the son. He *is*."). Tionna behaved similarly, when she countered Lyron's admiration of the singer Little Bow Wow with "He ugly. On my birthday I will say that—I will say it on the radio. [in high pitch voice] Little Bow wow is *so ugly. Yes he i::s."*

Such conversational skills, rooted in family and community life, reflect children's intricate knowledge of their home language's grammatical rules as well as their sensitivity to the communicative moment. To elaborate, complex linguistic rules govern when AAL speakers delete the copula (i.e., the forms of the verb *be*— *is* or *are*). The copula is more likely to be deleted when an adjective follows (e.g., "He ugly") rather than a noun phrase; it is also more likely to be absent when it follows a pronoun rather than a noun subject (e.g., "Little Bow Wow is *so ugly*"). (For discussion of these rules, see Rickford, 1999). And, as Monique and Tionna both illustrated, rhetorical and situational conditions may influence this grammatical action (see Scott, 1998).

Such communicative competence allows children to build social worlds in school. Moreover, children draw on their everyday discourse to literally find a way in to academic discussions. As Vygotsky (1962, p. 109) explained, children's "scientific concepts" develop as they are infused with, and support, children's reflections on everyday knowledge. In the following example, Ms. Hache, Mrs. Kay's student teacher, has been leading the children through a weekly newspaper activity sheet on "segregate" and "desegregate." In the world of the worksheet, these words translate as a group of same or differently colored children (literally). In the midst of their methodical movement through the sheet, Manuel breaks through the strict lesson structure, in which Ms. Hache asks a question, a child responds, and Ms. Hache evaluates (cf., Cazden, 2001; Mehan, 1979). Manuel asks a question, the discussion space opens up, and the pace quickens.

Manuel: What if we were still segregated?
Ms. Hache: What do you think, Manuel?

Manuel: It would be White kids in some schools and the Black kids in others.
Ms. Hache: . . . So where do you think you would be?
Manuel: In the Mexican school.
Mandisa: What about Chinese kids?
Ms. Hache: . . . Manuel said we would have a whole bunch of different schools. What do other people think? Tionna, what do you have to say?

Tionna's "mom" is her grandmother, who is relatively old. This may be behind Tionna's ability here to rethink the terms of the discussion:

Tionna: Those—What about those people that doesn't have moms? Their moms were old and stuff, what would they do? . . . What if there was a school for people that doesn't have moms?
Ms. Hache: . . . Tionna is saying what if we weren't segregated by color? What if we were segregated or separated by . . . family life? . . . Do you think that would be a good thing?
Tionna: 'Cause people, 'cause little kids that doesn't have moms and dads don't have nowhere to sleep and stuff. And they can stay at the school and bring their sleeping bags to sleep there. . . . So when it's morning time they can get up, and one side is for girls, one side for boys and restrooms and stuff.

Like Alice, Andy, and Kenneth in their talk with Ms. Yung, Tionna and her peers stretched their language and their thinking—and, perhaps, Ms. Hache's as well—as they brought to the school lesson on "segregation" their implicit knowledge about variation in children's named ethnicities and in children's family circumstances. This stretching was collaboratively accomplished as they listened to one another ("What about Chinese kids?" Mandisa had asked). Opening up the strict lesson structure may have allowed some children to become engaged in a more quick-paced event, a recommendation that may be particularly important for some African American children (Haight, 2002; Heath, 1983). Just as important can be the teacher's clearing a space for children who thrive in a slower-paced discussion, where they do not have to work so hard to get a conversational turn.

In the "segregation" discussion, the children's attention, and Ms. Hache's, was mainly on their ideas, not their grammar; Ms. Hache modeled, extended, and responded to the children but did not explicitly correct their grammar (unlike in the writing conferences). Nonetheless, Tionna's speech contains an "error" heard only when addressing teachers—the use of *doesn't* for a particular third-person-plural construction. (In our book, "errors" are signs of children's efforts to figure out language.)

Tionna used a linguistic element (i.e., *doesn't,* instead of *don't*) associated with more formal talk. In fact, young AAL-speaking schoolchildren do come to use more formal (and more standardized) features in school speech or literacy events involving the authoritative presentation of ideas (Adger & Wolfram, 2000). More broadly, young children develop social and linguistic flexibility through interacting in diverse social situations with others who control varied ways with words and, also, through opportunities to exercise agency over language choices (Clark, 2003; Youssef, 1993).

This sociolinguistic flexibility suggests the value of opportunities for children to deliberately stretch their communicative repertoire, particularly in play. As we will discuss at length in Chapter 4, playing children may appropriate ways of talking from all manner of familiar others. For example, Tionna herself appropriated a diversity of voices, including the discourse of a fast-food worker, a disciplining mother, a guiding teacher, and a rhythmic rapper, not to mention a "fake" girlfriend (writing love notes), a party giver (organizing invitee lists), and a thoughtful daughter (designing cards and rewriting a "Mom's Day" poem).

Children can also listen to, read, talk about, and enact a diversity of texts, among them, formal letters, playground rhymes, and literary dialogue in varied vernaculars (Delpit & Dowdy, 2002). Without such opportunities, children may develop the misperception that voices like theirs do not belong in stories.

Joining and Transforming Societal Dialogues

Children's sociolinguistic flexibility does not tend to be a major focus of early schooling. Languages and language varieties other than standardized English are generally viewed as problems, not as the basis of children's communicative repertoires. This view of languages and language varieties as problematic is not only or even mainly due to concerns about the ease of communication at school. Rather, it derives from concerns about "standards" and the *power* to set them and, also, to meet them. *Ain't* is not less clear than *isn't,* but its social reverberations are different. And this is why people are so intense, emotional, and ambivalent about some of the children's ways with words.

And this brings back into focus the ideology of language use, of children becoming participants in a stratified society full of voices (Bakhtin, 1981). As Smitherman (2006) argues, "Everybody goes through school, and it is in school that negative language attitudes are reinscribed and reaffirmed" (p. 138).

A suggestive example can be found in Tionna's school experiences. Her school, in the industrialized urban Midwest, served a large proportion of African American students, along with smaller percentages of Latino and White students. And yet, her teachers Mrs. Kay and Ms. Hache had no formal linguistic knowledge of language variation. Mrs. Kay was, though, under enormous pressure to meet the standards for Reading First schools, in which achievement tests were given for usage and other conventions. And despite the fact that Mrs. Kay was an engaging and regular reader of books to her children, she did not read books written in a community vernacular that was not a variant of standardized English. Indeed, in Mrs. Kay's room, as in the local Reading First guidelines themselves, the language ideology stressed "correct" English.

In this instructional context, Mrs. Kay was of two minds about Tionna's writing. On the one hand, by midwinter she judged her as clearly the best writer in the room because of the fluency and vividness of her prose; indeed, she thought Tionna's writing was strong precisely because "there's lots of talk" in her home. As will be illustrated in Chapter 5, Tionna often appropriated the voices of others in her daily journal entries and, also, infused those entries with the evaluative tone of her everyday storytelling. On the other hand, Mrs. Kay's editing sessions with Tionna, as with other children, focused on "fixing" basic matters like grammar. Recall, for example, her efforts with Tionna's "*i*s."

Tionna's own encounters with a story written in AAL suggests the consequences of officially ignoring the voices of children's everyday lives. At the end of the 1st-grade year Anne asked Tionna to read Lucille Clifton's *Three Wishes* (1992), written in AAL. In the book, Lena, a child out walking with her friend Victor, finds a penny with her birthday year—a lucky penny! After looking at the book, Tionna asked Anne to read the book to her. As Anne did so, Tionna became very involved in the story, commenting often on what had or would happen.

When Anne returned for a follow-up visit a year later, Tionna not only read the book herself, but she responded to it quite differently (see Dyson & Smitherman, in press). At first, she tripped over words, self-correcting from AAL to LWC, or standardized English. This is a common response of young AAL-speaking children, even if they do not have productive control over the "standardized" features (Goodman & Goodman, 2000; Sims, 1976). For example, Clifton wrote "Victor say," and Tionna read "Victor says," before self-correcting to "Victor say." But soon she was correcting not her reading, but the book. "'Victor say,'" she read, and then she commented, "'Victor says,' it's supposed to be."

As Tionna got into the story, this commenting stopped and, in fact, she even self-corrected her intonation so that the written AAL sounded right. *"What you gonna wish?"* Clifton wrote. And Tionna read, deliberately enunciating each word, "What will—What you gonna wish?" Then she reread the sentence, quickening the pace and adding a conversational intonation: "Whatcha gonna wish?"

Still, when Tionna was finished reading, and Anne asked her if she thought Lucille Clifton was a good writer, Tionna responded: "Kind of." "But," she said, "some words need to be fixed."

Clifton wrote a pretty good story, but she isn't saying it right—this is what Tionna seemed to have learned from school (cf., Bull, 1990). Her very reading of the book—her ability to switch between "he say" and "he says," her deliberate changing of intonation and rhythm when moving from "What will you wish?" to "Whatcha gonna wish?"—suggested Tionna's ear for voices and her sociolinguistic flexibility. There was the possibility of a different pedagogical story for Tionna but, given the lack of any official attention to, or value afforded to such code-switching, it is unclear how Tionna would come to value and extend her own potential sophistication as a communicator.

Imagine, though, that Tionna had had the opportunity to hear characters speak in picture books and poetry that captured diverse societal voices, including voices that sounded like her family members and her neighbors. Imagine too that talk about these voices had been a common feature of her classroom life. In such circumstances, Tionna's response to Clifton's writing might have been different. (A suggestive counterexample can be found in Dyson, 2003, pp. 187–188.)

TOWARD HIGHER, BROADER, AND MORE HUMAN(E) STANDARDS

The early childhood classrooms we know best are filled with the richly varied voices of the very young. Their voices collectively transform the classroom into a novel, as Bakhtin might say—a grand story in which the child characters, as speakers, have different developmental histories, varying cultural and linguistic heritages and, at any point in time, different social agendas. As readers of the classroom, we listen for individual voices as they respond to the world around them, socially connecting, communicating, and declaring their own presence, their own importance, in the social scene.

Into this complex classroom world may come highly regulated language curricula organized around institutional standards. We have no objection to the notion of standards, of what we as educators should work toward as reasonable goals for the very young. But current standards and mandated curricula can be troubling. As we have argued herein, too often they imagine an idealized generic child, against whom all children might be measured, and that child is learning a generic language at a generic pace. The "different" children might need "explicit" instruction so that they, too, might sound generic.

We argue that it is possible to reimagine language standards in the absence of a standard or generic child. Key to this reimagining are

- Basic respect for children's inherent powers as language learners

- Recognition that language is a tool for social participation, intellectual exploration, and personal expression
- Grasp of the politics of language

First, "normal" children learn language at different rates (Nelson, 2007). Moreover, they do not learn a "generic" language; rather, they learn particular variants or dialects of language(s). Further, they may learn multiple languages themselves as they move among different institutional and relational settings.

There is, then, no generic child, no generic language. There are children and languages. Through this book, we aim to support curricula and standards that appreciate children's language-learning powers (e.g., the linguistic insight undergirding their constructive errors, the complexity of deciding whether "errors" are just that). And we also support a basic goal of communicative flexibility, rather than the mastery of one language variety. A solid and fair curricular goal is to expand, not constrict, children's language.

Second, language is a tool for young children. Within their families, they have varying opportunities and demands on how they use language to join with others. They will have ways of engaging with adults and peers, of asserting themselves, of playing, praying, and telling stories. In schools, our capacities to assess and stretch children's language use are dependent upon children having rich opportunities to use language for varied audiences and purposes. Among such contexts are occasions to discuss interesting objects and experiences with their peers and teachers, to tell and write stories to diverse others, to dramatize varied roles and scenes, and to be an expert—that is, to teach. Children's intention to play, entertain, persuade, analyze, and explain for and with particular others—to construct social worlds—must exist, or there is no communicative situation, no understood problem for which speech is the solution.

Finally, whatever our goals, we must meet them within institutions that historically are oriented toward the language and language variants of the powerful. When we as educators do not address the multiplicity of language and language varieties in children's worlds, we are teaching them that educated people do not sound like members of their own families and neighborhoods. In this chapter, we have used as our object lesson children's use of variants of language devalued by the larger society, particularly African American Language.

As educators, we have particular responsibilities to children who speak devalued languages. Moreover, we have responsibilities to teach all children about the aesthetics of literary and artful language use and to prepare them for a global society. Thus, in addition to "modeling standard English," as those California guidelines suggest, adults who explicitly model language flexibility may be particularly valuable in the early years, as may books in which people speak in varied ways. Given that we live in a society of many accents and dialects, such exposure to and knowledge about language varieties is important for all children.

Indeed, it is interesting that there has been no voiced concern about children whose home language is considered a standard English. What sort of democracy can we have if children, influenced by their elders, learn to dismiss some voices out of hand (and out of mind)? How can children understand our history, our current social struggles, and our literature without an appreciation of our changing languages? How prepared will children be for participation in an emerging world order in which there are increasing varieties of English around the globe?

In the opening vignettes, Lyron and Ezekial were managing their social world by managing language use. The point herein is that the children's continued growth as language learners entails—yes—learning new ways with words, but also using their developing social (and power-related) astuteness to engage as flexible participants in ever-expanding worlds.

3. Diverse Language Learners in Diverse Times

When the "Norm" Isn't English

In Chapter 2 we focused on varieties of English, concluding that a single "standard" is completely out of step with the world as it now is. Next we turn to early childhood classrooms where many children start the school year without a knowledge of English. These are places, like the Head Start classroom you encountered in Chapter 1, where the so-called norm is not a variety of English. There, one teacher and many of the children spoke Spanish, though some, like Luisa, at first did not. Recall that sitting quietly with an upside-down book in hand, she was the youngest child in the room—not quite 3 years of age—and she spent much of her first year watching a lot and talking little. Learning her way around a Head Start classroom, she was surrounded by children who were generally more talkative than she but who shared a specific potential: the potential to become multilingual.

This chapter focuses on children who demonstrate that potential in a variety of ways over time—following diverse developmental time lines. Luisa was one who took her time: A bit more than a year after the upside-down-book event, she was central to this interaction at the sand table in a Head Start room for 4-year-olds, where her classmates have noticed—sometimes with surprise—a much more talkative and engaged Luisa:

Luisa has found a button and brought it to the sand table.

> *Luisa:* Lookit, I found it.
> *Josué: Dame, dame.* (Give me, give me.)
> *Luisa:* I want to play.
> *Josué:* You want to play? (sounding surprised) Someone stop.
>   Luisa wants to play.
> *Josué and Sarine:* Miguel is done.
> *Luisa:* I play, I play! (said with animation and some adamance).

We elaborate below on the paths that Luisa and four other young children took as they became multilingual and moved from speaking the language of their families to the language(s) of schooling, Spanish and English for Luisa and her friends and English for other children. We next include a bit of the children's broad, societal context.

THE SOCIETAL CONTEXT FOR MULTILINGUAL LEARNING

The five children highlighted in this chapter are members of families that are seeking a place for themselves in the always-shifting terrain of a new city in a new country (for one example, see Smith, 2006, for a rich ethnographic account of families of Mixteco heritage in New York City and Mexico). The families of the five children have varied labels attached to them: African-American, African-Caribbean, Haitian; Asian, Asian-American, Chinese; Hispanic, Mexican, Mexican-American; and so on. All families share the label of "immigrant" or, as we prefer, "newcomer."

Educators refer to children learning English or a language not used at home in a variety of ways: English learners (ELs), English language learners (ELLs), English as a second language (ESL) students, or emergent bilinguals (EBs) (Garcia, Kleifgen, & Falchi, 2008); and in the English-centric words of the federal government, limited English proficient (LEP). In referring to the children in this chapter, we will use the positive term *emergent bilinguals* (EBs) in order to mark and appreciate their potential to learn more than one language—English or another language—and to emphasize that the language(s) being learned emerge over time.

EBs are the most rapidly growing population in U.S. schools. In the 10 years between 1993 and 2003, the share of EBs at elementary and secondary schools increased by over 50%, from 2.8 to more than 4 million children (Cosentino de Cohen, Deterding, & Clewell, 2005, p. 2). Moreover, an analysis of data from the 2000 census reveals that 20% of all children in the United States have at least one parent who is an immigrant or newcomer. Recent analyses reveal, too, how quickly these families in all 50 states establish U.S. roots (Hernandez, Denton, & Macartney, 2007). For example, 80% of children in newcomer families are born in the United States; and according to their parents, about 74% of them between birth and 17 years of age are fluent in English, while 46% of them speak another language at home. Preschool-age children in these families are less likely than children in nonnewcomer families to attend preschool, despite the fact that the number of EBs in Head Start and public pre-kindergartens is increasing. The availability of pre-kindergartens varies by geographic region or state so young children living in certain states may lack early opportunities to become multilingual in group settings.

In short, the number of families in the United States with complex demographic and linguistic histories is increasing, not just in urban areas, which one would expect to be diverse, but also in suburban and rural areas. Unfortunately public perception of EBs of all ages continues to be negative. Note, for example, ads in locales like New York City for "accent-reduction classes," intended to make EBs more employable, or a petition from townspeople in Massachusetts who protested the hiring of an elementary-school teacher with an "accent" ("Humanities 101," 1992). Children learning English are also seen as "others" or speakers of "other" languages, who may be referred to special education classes, as if lack of knowledge of English is in itself a learning disability. The resources of potentially multilingual learners like Luisa are sometimes disregarded. In contrast we, like the teacher in *First Grade Takes a Test,* want to emphasize what children are able to do. Thus we assert that knowledge of an additional language or dialect is a rich resource, unrecognized by the typical standardized test, and that it is simply wrong to equate linguistic "difference" or "diversity" with inability or deficit (García, 2005; Genishi, 2002).

In this chapter we foreground this aspect of sociolinguistic flexibility: the potential of young children to become multilingual. We present the abilities and linguistic resources of five children between the ages of 3 and 6, who participate in multilingual communication in particular social and educational contexts. Each demonstrates an individual approach and rate of learning: Tommy and Pierre are sketched briefly and, because they contrast with each other, they help us present a theoretical framework for considering EBs in general. We introduce Miguel and Luisa in more detail as they move from Head Start to kindergarten classrooms. Finally, Alice demonstrates her abilities from pre-K to 1st grade, showing consistent interests at intersections of language, literacy, and science. Alice, Luisa, and Miguel, all with unique "inner clocks," take their time to become speakers; and over time their bilingualism emerges in distinctive ways.

PARTICULAR CHILDREN IN PARTICULAR CLASSROOMS: CONTRASTING STORIES

Tommy, Speaker of Cantonese, Then English

Tommy and Pierre are both EBs who appear to draw from the same reservoir of high energy. You can hear more from Tommy in Chapter 5 and elsewhere, as his is a distinctive voice in Donna Yung-Chan's public school pre-kindergarten (pre-K) where many children and Ms. Yung speak Cantonese (Genishi, Stires, & Yung-Chan, 2001; Genishi, Yung-Chan, & Stires, 2000). We include him here as an example of a rapid language learner. He speaks Cantonese with his family members, mainly his mother and grandparents, and starts the school year speaking only Cantonese.

Because he appears to become an English speaker with little effort, there are few vignettes of Tommy as a silent bystander. Indeed *silent* is an adjective that one would not attach to his name. His hand is usually up during morning meeting— he is constantly ready to express himself. A quick scan of transcripts of videotapes of Ms. Yung's room shows his regular and frequent contributions in whole-group, teacher-directed activities and small-group, child-initiated times. By April of the pre-K year, for example, Tommy is showing his friend, Ashley, how to measure the length of her hand, as opposed to the length of her thumb, with connected colored plastic cubes. With emphasis, he instructs with words and gestures, "Not! Not this one! You're supposed to do *this!*" At the end of the school year in June, he is central to a bit of quick-paced dialogue at activity time, as he and his friends, whose home language is also Cantonese, playfully share markers:

> *Tommy:* I want a green.
> *Jeffrey:* You take blue! No, this is green!
> *Tommy:* I need to use that.
> *Tommy:* I use this.
> *Ashley:* Here's blue.
> *Jeffrey:* I bet this is a better color.
> *Tommy:* You got to say thank you. Black and blue floating through the
> breeze! K, k, k, k. No. What are you doing? (He asks Jeffrey.)

Tommy is one of the few EBs in this classroom who is able to write alphabet letters and play so facilely in English, demonstrating his ability to learn a second language quickly. This does not mean that he sounds like a child whose primary language was English. English speakers would say he has a slight "accent" and that his syntax is occasionally not Englishlike, but his fluency makes his mistakes negligible.

Pierre, Speaker of Haitian-Creole, Then English

In a very different classroom from Tommy's, Pierre also starts the year speaking his home language rather than English. He is one of 31 children in an English-as-a-Second-Language (ESL) public kindergarten, where all the children have been categorized as "ESL" and came from eight different language backgrounds (Fassler, 2003). The teacher, Mrs. Barker, was originally from Wales, and to North American ears sounds British; she is the only one in the room whose primary language is English.

Like many children learning a second language, Pierre is eager to communicate. In the beginning of the year, he uses pantomime and sound effects to participate in group times that focus on topics like the letter of the week (Fassler, 2003). Pierre appears to interpret the event as a drama and, for example, provides airplanelike droning sounds when Mrs. Barker mentions airplanes. Or he makes the sound of squealing brakes when she talks about slowing down at traffic lights.

Over time Pierre begins to use words instead of sounds, helpfully synchronizing "woof, woof, woof, woof" with Mrs. Barker's use of a hand puppet, a brown dog. A few months later, Pierre is less a dramatic accompanist and more of an attentive student. The teacher has been doing read-alouds of books like Kightley's *Opposites* (1986) to teach vocabulary. According to Fassler (2003, pp. 51–52):

> By this time, Pierre's incorporation of the teacher's vocabulary was consistently evident in his pattern of ending the discussion of specific pairs of opposites with a statement of the pair. Here are two of many examples:
>
> > *T* (teacher): In—
> > *Janine:* and out.
> > *T:* Yes. He's going in and coming out.
> > *Pierre:* In and out. In and out.
> > *T:* This sheep is—
> > *Children:* Big. (Then T points to the small one.) Little.
> > *T:* Or small. Yes, *little* is what it says.
> > *Pierre:* Big 'n small. Big 'n small.

In time Mrs. Barker insists that Pierre say exactly what is written in the text; for example, if the text is "long dog," she tells him, "long dog," which he then repeats.

WEAVING RESEARCH AND THEORY TOGETHER WITH CHILDREN'S LANGUAGE-AND-ACTION WAYS

How is it that individuals accomplish a feat like learning a new language within a framework that links distinctive children like Pierre and Tommy together? Or put in Marie Clay's (1998) terms, how do we account for the "different paths" by which learners reach the common outcome of learning a second language? In both Ms. Yung's and Mrs. Barker's rooms children take their own paths, marching to the rhythm of their own inner clocks, not abandoning their ways of making sense in the face of a language they don't speak. Like children learning their primary language, the EBs work toward shared meanings with teachers who enable the pairing of language or languages with actions. Fassler analyzes Pierre's progress in English in terms of his trademark "language-and-action ways" (Lindfors, 1999) of turning to the topic at hand (Fassler, 2003) and learning to attend to the teacher and share the teacher's meanings and those of written texts—specifically, the way Pierre moves from action (miming and sound effects) to language in dramatized action (saying "woof, woof" on the dog puppet's behalf) to language (articulating opposites like *big* and *small*). Many children's language learning is less audible, visible, and dramatic than Pierre's. Yet both he and Tommy, who learned to speak English more quickly than his pre-K peers, and Pierre, effectively pair language with action and the use of objects to become participants in the social worlds around them. Both boys are in classrooms where their teachers know how to allow for and expand on the EBs' varied language-and-action ways.

As we noted in Chapter 2, children's seemingly inborn abilities to detect patterns in language may lead to EBs' use of language forms that reflect features of both their home language and the language of schooling. In Tommy's case some of these features—or "mistakes," from an adult viewpoint—are syntactic or grammatical and phonological, although the number of "mistakes" are minute in number compared to the amount of English he has learned. Because of each learner's sociocultural characteristics and individual language-and-action ways, there will always be more variation and difference than sameness within any group of EBs.

In the face of this ever-growing variation, we also acknowledge the theoretical umbrellas that account for the ways in which individuals are alike. Recall that in Chapter 2, we referred to language learning as grounded in our humanness, in our biology (Chomsky, 1965; Pinker, 1994). Further, we highlighted the essential social interactions, regardless of cultural context, in which language is learned (Nelson, 2007; Vygotsky, 1978). And as we noted earlier and as Bakhtin (1981) explained, language is by nature not an individual phenomenon or accomplishment; it exists in dialogue. Something said or written is not meant to dangle in conversational space; rather, it invites a response from another or others. Thus our theoretical umbrella contains some universal spokes that underlie the learning of any language:

- First, we assert that almost all persons learn their primary or home language by virtue of being human, not through direct instruction by adults.

- Second, children learn language, on whatever path at whatever rate, on a social plane. Language learning comes through countless interactions with others across varied sociocultural contexts.
- Third, language exists in dialogue with others. Something articulated—said or written—is an invitation for response from others.

We next present in some detail Luisa, Miguel, and Alice, three young EBs whose particular accomplishments show them to be different from Tommy, Pierre, and each other, while they all fit under the theoretical umbrella just described.

PRE-KINDERGARTNERS BECOMING LANGUAGE LEARNERS IN HEAD START: TAKING THEIR TIME

Nobody sees a flower, really—it is so small—we haven't time, and to see takes time, like to have a friend takes time.

—Georgia O'Keeffe

In the late fall of 2005 Ariela Zycherman and Celia started a study in which we asked how some pre-kindergartners become communicators in a Head Start center for 3- and 4-year-olds. The children, like flowers, are in fact small when they first enter their classrooms. The growth of their knowledge of languages and literacy creates a story over time, after many events and interactions in the larger context of what they, their peers, and their teachers do. In this section we focus on two children who take their time to become communicators—and to make friends.

The Educational and Sociolinguistic Context

The broad educational context for the focal children is the federally funded Head Start program, established in 1965 as part of President Lyndon Johnson's Great Society (Powell, 2005). In addition to helping preschool children from families with low incomes "catch up" academically with economically advantaged peers, Head Start has emphasized parent participation. After the establishment of the Good Start, Grow Smart initiative (2002), however, there has been less emphasis on the communitarian aspects of Head Start and an increased emphasis on early reading skills. Despite this unfortunate shift toward academic goals, the Head Start we observed maintains its commitment to a play-based curriculum, as you will see below.

Most of the children in the Head Start classrooms we observed are of Mexican heritage, and their parents are recent newcomers to New York City.

In the 3s room when we begin the study, there are six children whose families are speakers of Mixteco, an indigenous language in areas of the states of Guerrero, Oaxaca, and Puebla in south-central and western Mexico. We choose to focus on these six children, with their potential for multilingualism, and the next fall follow them into the 4s rooms. Within each room children range from being monolingual in English or Spanish, bilingual in both, or emerging as bilinguals in English or Spanish. A few of the children start out the year as Mixteco speakers or spoke Mixteco at home; and for them Spanish is their second language and English is their third. Hence the suitability of the descriptor *multilingual.*

In the 3s and 4s rooms that we observed the head teachers are English speakers, and the assistant teachers or coteachers are Spanish-dominant but bilingual in Spanish and English. The curriculum is quite open-ended, and the teachers describe it as play-based, within the required Head Start structure of HighScope (Hohmann, Banet, & Weikart, 1979), with its phases of *planning* what children are going to do, *doing* those things, and later *reviewing,* or telling the group what they did. The teachers and the center's education director all mention the importance of social and emotional development in the context of their curriculum. Thus, in the field of early childhood, they would say their curriculum is compatible with "developmentally appropriate practice" (Bredekamp & Copple, 1997).

So in a room where most children do not speak English and the teachers try to provide appropriate curriculum, there is no general expectation that children will communicate in English. Head teacher Fran does not have this expectation for the 3s in her room, and so, once again, because individual children come to the classroom with varied histories, they show much more sociolinguistic variation than uniformity. Moreover, Fran and her assistant teacher Lana have flexible expectations, within a flexible curriculum. In other words, their rooms are *inclusive* (Grisham-Brown, Hemmeter, & Pretti-Frontczak, 2005)—children are accepted as they are and are given time to learn and adapt to the new setting of preschool. Although a few children eventually receive services for special needs, most do not. Teachers patiently anticipate the emergence of the children's abilities, not disabilities.

Miguel and Luisa: Two Different Paths

In this section we focus on two of the six focal children in the ongoing study, Miguel and Luisa, who spend part of their first year in the 3s room beginning to speak Spanish. Adults might call both 3-year-olds "loners" who seldom communicate verbally. Although they seem unlikely as choices for a case study of EBs' oral language learning, they allow us to focus on the varied ways in which they communicate and become familiar with their first school setting. Indeed, they show a kinship with Pierre in Mrs. Barker's room as he moved into spoken English by first relying on actions and objects.

In Figure 3.1 we present chronologically and side by side word sketches, selectively drawn from field notes spanning more than a year. Although there are a small number of sketches, rather like slices of communicative histories, both children demonstrate that they take their own paths, set their own pace, and make their own choices. (These sketches may remind you of anecdotal records that you have written as you observe and assess informally in the classroom. See Chapter 6 for more on this kind of assessment.) You will see that neither Luisa nor Miguel would be called talkative or sociable in the 3s room, but each has particular ways of communicating nonverbally and verbally. Further, each has a distinctive way of participating in the pre-K curriculum from one year to the next. After the last word sketches from February of 2007 of the 4s year, the two children become talkative enough that word-sketches fail to do justice to their language, actions, and interactions. Like Tommy and Pierre, Miguel and Luisa provide a contrast and have language-and-action ways of gradually turning toward their teachers' curriculum (Fassler, 2003; Lindfors, 1999).

Miguel: Preferring Action and Objects to Talk. Particularly during the 3s year Miguel is a child who does not call attention to himself with peers or with adults, as he seldom initiates interactions. He appears to understand whatever is said in Spanish, and usually in response to Lana and Fran, he makes minimal utterances. What he chooses to attend to, as Clay (1998, p. 85) would say, is usually his favorite *área de bloques* (block area) where he builds elaborate roads and buildinglike structures. For weeks at a time, at least during our twice-a-week visits, he devotes most of his energies to playing with blocks and trucks. He has occasional conflicts with other children when he is unwilling to share materials. He continues to softly answer teachers' questions and produces sound effects while playing in the block area. Unlike kindergartner Pierre, he does not synchronize his sound effects with others' language, as his play scenes are his own.

By April of the 3s year, Miguel is speaking more Spanish, but his utterances, for example, *"Yo voy a jugar"* ("I'm going to play") are sometimes followed by mumbles. His sound effects (roaring vehicle sounds, "beep beep") are as meaningful as his words. Thus his language-and-action ways convey meaning to others via some spoken language, sound effects, and quite a bit of action.

FIGURE 3.1. Word Sketches Over Time of EBs Miguel and Luisa

MIGUEL	LUISA
The 3s Year	

November 2005	*November 2005*
Played alone; did not attempt to play with others. Nodded answers to questions from teachers like "*Quieres leche?*" (Do you want milk?). During planning answered that he was playing with *carros* (cars).	Played alone; tried to follow other girls around but was unsuccessful in trying to play with them. She did not answer any questions during planning time.
A few days later:	*Two weeks later:*
Josué spilled his milk during breakfast, and Miguel said, "Lana!" (coteacher). Then mumbled something until he got her attention. During planning he said his paintbrush was "yellow" and said he was going to play in the *área de familia, cocinando solo* (family area, cooking by himself).	She said her name when it was her turn to at the beginning of the day. During planning she did not answer with words but pointed to the *área de familia* (family area) and nodded yes to painting and no to *caballos* (horses), or plastic animals. The rest of the hour she made a collage with girls at the table. She did not speak.

January 2006	*January 2006*
Did not talk during breakfast. Said his pom pom was *blanco* when Fran (teacher) said the word. Mumbled that he would play in *área de bloques,* then something inaudible. Had a fake sword fight with Ana and played with trucks alone.	During planning Luisa very quietly said her pompom was *morado* (purple). It was actually *marrón* (brown). Then she quietly said she would play in the *área de familia* and *sí*. She played with fake money (what the other girls were doing), and she responded "yes" and "no" to many of Fran's questions during play time.

February 2006	*February 2006*
During planning Miguel is quiet. What he said was not audible. Played with planes in block area. Stacked trucks and made "beep beep" noises. Marco came over to play with him, but the two played near each other, not with each other. . . . During recall he would not talk on the phone, as the teachers requested, as a way of varying recall time.	Absent at beginning of month. Second week of month she repeated after teacher *tortuga* (turtle) and *verde* (green). Played by herself, usually with table toys. Third week of month nodded in response to Lana's questions about what she wants at breakfast. Said *área de familia* (family area) during planning. Played in family area, then with table toys, and wandered around.
	March 2006
	At the playground. Luisa talked with Brian under the slide. Other children were going up and down the slide and running around. Miguel and Luisa occasionally ran around the playground with others.

April 2006	*April 2006*
Miguel said his pom pom was *azul* (blue), which it was, and *yo voy a jugar* (I am going to play), but what followed was inaudible.	Luisa said some things extremely quietly and said them on her own. She said her pom pom was *rosado* (pink), which it was. She said, "*Yo voy a jugar en área de familia*" (I am going to play in the family area). Played with Monique and her friends, mainly following them, but with more interaction than before.

(continued)

MIGUEL	LUISA

The 4s Year

October 2006	*October 2006*

Sam was talking to Miguel. Miguel, Sam, and Anthony talked about having three pieces of French toast each, and each said he could eat all of them.

Miguel hit Anthony with a block. Dominga (coteacher) asked what happened, and Miguel said, "*Yo quiero jugar con los bloques, y él viene a jugar*" (I want to play with the blocks, and he comes to play). Dominga said, "*Y no quieres que él juega contigo?*" (And you don't want him to play with you?). Miguel said, "No."

Miguel said, "*No me gusta*" (I don't like it) when Dominga told him to eat something. Then she said something about not talking with his mouth full. *Miguel:* "Eh?" *Dominga:* "*Porque está mejor masticar la comida. Coma primero y luego me dice.*" (Because it's better to chew your food. Eat first and then tell me.) *Miguel:* "Eh?" *Dominga:* "*Coma primero y luego me dice*" (Eat first and then tell me).

Luisa got up to get a cup, and Rebeca passed her the milk. And then Luisa said "*No quiero leche, quiero fruta*" (I don't want milk, I want fruit). She took a cup back to her seat and gave herself fruit. She was the only one who ate it.

Luisa had trouble opening the door to the bathroom. After Josué opened the door and blocked her way, Dominga and Josué both asked her, "*Qué dices?*" (What do you say?), repeating "*Qué dices?*". Eventually Luisa said, "*Gracias*" (Thank you).

January 2007	*January 2007*

Miguel got a cup from Pat (teacher) so he could brush his teeth. After she gave him the cup, he said slowly in a loud, clear voice, "Thank you, Pat!"

At the end of the month Miguel played with Carolina at the computer. He had been talking with Anthony in English in the block area. He threw two planes into a cubbie and said, "I got two!"

In the kitchen area Carolina gave Luisa the phone and said, "*Es tu mamá*" (It's your mom). Luisa took it and talked. They smiled and talked very quietly and handed the phone back and forth to each other.

A week later:

Luisa, Tina, and Carolina played with a roller suitcase, and Luisa said, "*Dámelo*" (Give it to me) as they filled it with plastic toys. Imani joined them as they stuffed the suitcase. They had a conversation in Spanish about how much was in the suitcase. Luisa started off by saying, "*Es mucho, verdad?*" (It's a lot, right?).

February 2007	*February 2007*

Miguel: Look, Anthony. I am going to show you.

Anthony took a plastic figure and said "I took one."

Miguel: Dámelo (Give it to me).
Anthony: No.
Miguel: Give it me.
Anthony: No.
Miguel: I am going to hurt you. I am going to get you. Hurry, get in my car.

Luisa and Rebeca played across the table from each other. Rebeca called to Luisa and she responded "Luis-o." This went on back and forth. Rebeca brought observer (Ariela) a pot of plastic figures/people and told her it was a *dulce* (dessert). Ariela asked, "*Dulce de gente?*" (People dessert?) and Rebeca laughed. Then Luisa brought Ariela a plate with beads on it. Ariela asked what it was. Luisa said, "Jello." Ariela asked what flavors, and Luisa said, "Purple, red, yellow, and green." Ariela said her favorite is purple, and Luisa said her favorite is orange. (There was an orange bead on the plate.)

Luisa: Watching and Taking Her Time. As our notes show, in the 3s Room Luisa says little for quite a long time, so that some observers might say that she is in a prolonged "silent period" (Tabors, 1997). In fact she is virtually silent only in the first few weeks after her arrival, but for the first year what she says can easily be recorded by hand, as her utterances are short and, at least while we are present, infrequent.

By January of the 1st year Luisa responds with single words and phrases in response to Fran and Lana and often chooses table toys like puzzles. She seems observant and sometimes moves from area to area on her own. By March we observe her talking to Brian under the slide at the park, and she and Miguel occasionally participate in chase games. Thus, although neither she nor Miguel is viewed as sociable, they engage in some social activities, but not always together. By April Luisa can use "complete sentences"—something the teachers encourage—to announce what she plans to do. For example, "*Yo voy a jugar en área de familia*" ("I'm going to play in the family area"). She begins to play with some of the girls, and by the summer she participates briefly in conversations. Throughout the year both she and Miguel are learning school vocabulary, like colors in Spanish.

Miguel and Luisa in the 4s Room. In the fall of their 4s year both Miguel and Luisa are speaking in longer utterances and more often. Miguel still favors the block area and so talks occasionally to Sam and Anthony, who also favor block play. Conflicts are more frequent, and he explains why he hit someone, in this case Anthony, in a straightforward way: "*Yo quiero jugar con los bloques, y él viene a jugar*" ("I want to play with the blocks, and he comes to play").

Luisa speaks in more developed ways than she did in the 3s room, saying things like "*No quiero leche, quiero fruta*" ("I don't want milk, I want fruit"). She also shows resistance to Josué when he insists that she say "*gracias*" to him for opening the bathroom door for her. She eventually accedes to Josué with a quick "*gracias,*" following the politeness rule that teachers consistently model and articulate. In November there are few notes about Luisa; she is absent from time to time.

By January of the 4s year Luisa seems suddenly transformed into a talker. We observe her in the family/kitchen area having pretend phone chats and talking about the objects she and other girls are playing with. She has friends and sometimes is able to determine the direction of play. For the first time we hear her playing with language; for example, with her name, changing it to *Luis-o* and then making a game of chanting it with her good friend Rebeca.

Luisa's story is incomplete without a drama that is unrelated to her play and unexplained in our notes. According to her mother, in November of the 4s year Luisa has surgery on one of her ears, following a number of infections. The teachers concur that Luisa's mom talked to them in the past about ear infections, that they recommended a hearing test for Luisa, and that especially after the winter break in December, Luisa spoke for herself in a new way, proclaiming—you'll recall—"I play! I play!"

Everyone happily concludes that the surgery for her hearing impairment determined the timing of Luisa's announcement. Yet it's hard to assess just how the impairment affected her language-learning process. Her language is such that we guess she was hearing well for quite a while before the surgery since she was speaking clearly articulated Spanish and English soon after the surgery. Our guess, too, is that in her early months in the 3s room Luisa may have been quiet, but not at all passive. She was comprehending, taking it all in, and laying the foundation for the moment when she could hear and be heard, loud and clear. The story of the successful intervention illustrates another way in which the Head Start teachers are inclusive, how they share information with Luisa's mom about services for special needs, yet continue to see Luisa as a child with a particular style and abilities that will emerge.

Nothing this dramatic happens to Miguel, but by January he is heard clearly speaking English to the head teacher, Pat—"Thank you, Pat!"—and with his friends in the block area. So the language histories of Miguel and Luisa follow different arcs. Their different language-and-action ways of communicating and interacting suggest that they are on parallel paths, particularly with respect to Luisa's emphatic entry into sociodramatic play, to which we will return in Chapter 4. After a year in their 4s room, they speak with ease in Spanish, the language of the surrounding community; and Miguel is beginning to show his bilingual abilities in Spanish and English. By late spring of that year, Luisa is also speaking some English, appropriately with Pat, the English-speaking teacher, and girls who speak almost exclusively in English.

Luisa is fluent enough in English that Pat speaks to her in English about her plans. Luisa says she will play in the sand area, but Pat corrects her:

Pat: It's not sand; it's water now.
Luisa: I want to play in the water. And I want to play in the area, in the art area. And I want to play with Imani (English speaker). And I want to play with that.
Pat: What?
Luisa: Paint.

Miguel switches from Spanish to English while giving instructions to Anthony, an English speaker who spoke a little Spanish, for building something with blocks:

Miguel: Y pone éste allí (And put this one there). Oh remember yesterday you put it like that, and it went like that.

Luisa and Miguel construct "complete sentences" in Spanish and English, occasionally deviating in small ways from conventional adultlike forms. For example, while pretending, Miguel says, "He broke with the block," instead of "He broke it [his hand] with the block." And Luisa says, "She put this [cereal] on chair," leaving out *the* before *chair*.

Over time, and with a medical intervention, Luisa has become a player who can play in large part because she can say more. Miguel, in contrast, can clearly say more but is less engaged at this time in establishing friendships. The remarkable progress of both children has occurred over a period of a year and a half. We come back to the importance of this extended period of time later in the chapter.

KINDERGARTEN:
THE EMERGENCE OF BILITERACY

By the winter and spring of the focal children's kindergarten year, our collaborative research group had grown to include Ysaaca Axelrod and Lorraine (Lori) Falchi, who join in observing children in two dual-language classrooms. The children had started their transition into public school in the fall and into the more formalized literacy practices of kindergarten.

Miguel and Luisa have been placed in different classrooms, both designated as "dual language" in a public school in a largely Latino neighborhood. The term *dual language* refers to a kind of curriculum offered at a small number of schools, and it means that the school values the children's abilities to learn and maintain more than one language. Thus Spanish and English are used by days of the week, two days in Spanish and two days in English, with Spanish and English alternating on Fridays. In practice teachers occasionally used the "other" language to make their communications clear to all the children. The children in general tend to speak the language they speak most fluently and the language of the person whom they are addressing. Luisa and Miguel code-switch, or alternate between Spanish and English, and seem more fluent in Spanish than English. That is, Spanish seems to be their language of choice when playing or speaking with peers. The next sections show how they behave and perform as early readers in a school that emphasizes literacy learning as much as it does bilingual abilities.

As Luisa, Miguel, and their Head Start classmates move into kindergarten, they encounter a balanced literacy program that in this school uses children's literature, music, writing, art, and occasionally drama to build a community of readers and writers. Miguel's teacher, Ms. Valdez, enacts balanced literacy in a way that adheres to the reading/writing workshop model (Calkins, 2003), supplemented by a hybrid model of explicit instruction in phonemic awareness (understanding that speech is made up of individual sounds) in Spanish. Luisa's teacher, Ms. de Luna, in contrast, focuses on literacy, but also offers an array of activities that would be associated with the "language arts." For instance, she regularly engages the children in singing and reciting poetry and stories, as well as in reading aloud. Indeed she often says that developing children's memories—"*la memoria*"—is central to their learning. She expresses frustration with the required curriculum, stating that kindergartners are not ready for so much reading and writing.

Both teachers are pressured by the dominant testing discourse, which is most evident toward the end of the academic year when children are tested in reading. Throughout the year teachers feel anxious about displaying their students' work in portfolios and on bulletin boards. Despite adults' anxiety, the children are generally responsive to the curriculum, which offers some child choice in both classrooms, as we see next.

Luisa, a Reader of the Classroom, Still Watchful

In the 3s room, Luisa was notably quiet and remarkably watchful. As a kindergartner she is hardly voluble and remains observant, sometimes watching her teacher, Ms. de Luna, intently for cues as to what she is supposed to do or say. When called on, she usually responds appropriately to questions like these:

What day of the week is it?
What is the first month of the year?
Good morning (the beginning of a song, which Luisa can sing).

Luisa is able to respond orally, as well as read and track words, one by one, sometimes as the class is singing a song like "New York, New York." She can also read and point to words such as "I am a lion. I can jump." In Spanish she writes sentences like "*Yo me baño*" (I take a bath) or "*Yo me peino*" (I comb my hair). These writing activities often consist of cloze sentences so that the teacher provides the opening words ("*Yo me . . .*") and the children fill in the last word on their own. In many cases the teacher says the word, and the children then spell it on their own.

Luisa generates beginning and ending sounds, sometimes syllables, and with help sounds out words correctly. She can do this independently, using invented spelling, as she does with a list of clothing:

casa (*camisa*—shirt or blouse)
fa (*falda*—skirt)
p (*pantalones*—pants).

Later in the school year, with scaffolding, she writes a poem in English, as part of a unit in their reading/writing curriculum:

I like brbs (I like barbies).
I like to play with my str (I like to play with my sister).
I hv lr brbs (I have lots of barbies).

An adult tutor's scaffolding includes questions like, "What do you like about barbies?" and later, "What else about barbies? Do you have one or do you have a lot?" Also, Luisa is encouraged to sound out, "What's at the end of *play?*" She has stopped after *p-l,* and the classmate next to her has just sounded out the *a,* with the tutor's help. The tutor also tells the children about the final *y.* We cannot help but note that Luisa is now writing about playing at home, rather than declaring herself a player, as she did in the 4s room. She is still a player in kindergarten, but like Miguel, she plays around the edges of the curriculum.

Ariela wrote this as an end-of-year summary about Luisa, still quiet and developing as a good student who makes choices about what to do:

Luisa is doing very well and sits at a table with some of the more advanced bilingual students in the class. She has one or two close friends whom she talks to, but generally she is pretty quiet. She follows directions well, but when her table is doing something (right or wrong), she does what they do. Luisa seems to challenge herself or maybe indulge herself to do slightly more difficult work if it has a picture or a word she likes, and she wants to work with it. She rarely raises her hand to be called up in front of the class.

Miguel, a Reader Who Still Plays

Our view of Miguel in pre-kindergarten was of a child who seldom played with others, but who was already demonstrating his bilingualism by the end of the 4s year. When the context shifts from an open-ended, play-based curriculum to a notably literacy-based one, Miguel appears to adapt. According to Lori and Ysaaca, by February he is able to share orally in class, recognize letters of the alphabet and about half the letter sounds in English and in Spanish, and read and write simple sentences in Spanish.

Miguel still chooses to attend to tasks in his own way, in his own time. For example, he often does not complete his word-study work during the allotted time, so he has to finish it during choice time before he can play. Unlike many of his peers who socialize at the table and share their work with one another, he is very focused on completing his own work. When the teacher dictates a sentence containing the word-study words, among others, Miguel looks at the words, which he has written earlier on his paper, or at the word wall, repeating the words to himself slowly. He does not sound the words out, letter by letter. His penmanship is careful, and he rereads his sentences once they are written.

He also occasionally engages in creative writing, as when he writes a songlike poem about his friendship with Josué, a friend from Head Start. (Conventional Spanish spellings, then English translations are in parentheses):

> *Yo soi (soy) su* (I am his)
> *amgo (amigo) Di (de)* (friend of)
> *Josue (Josué)*
> *Yo si soi* (Yes I am)
> *su amgo* (his friend)
> *con Jose (Josué)* (with Josué)
> *Yo me une* (joined with?)
> *soi amgo Di Jose* (Josué)
> *sha sha sha.*

Ariela's brief summary of Miguel at year's end captures a child who is not highly sociable (but has at least one good friend) and is quite verbally creative:

> Miguel rarely participates in rug time and usually sits slightly apart from the group and looks around. But when he does participate, he tells long stories in Spanish. These stories usually consist of long sentences with three or four ideas where words like *y* (and), *después* (afterwards), and *entonces* (then) connect and extend the story. Comparatively, many of the other children give a one-sentence or less answer. During reading time Miguel is paired with Amy, and he reads extremely well, pointing to the words, speaking loudly and clearly. They also work well as a pair and often correct each other. When Miguel reads alone, he doesn't pay as close attention to the text and often plays with his books rather than reading them.

This paragraph, like the one Ariela wrote about Luisa, captures but a slice—really a sliver—of what both children are able to do sociolinguistically at the end of their kindergarten year. Move back in time and memory to the fall of their quiet 3s year, though, and consider how stunning their social, bilingual, and biliterate progress has been, the kind of progress that is also reflected in the upcoming story of Alice, whom you met briefly in Chapter 2.

A DIFFERENT PATH
OF CHANGE AND CONSISTENCY

In 1997 a 4-year-old named Alice joined a public pre-K classroom in New York's Chinatown. The full story about Alice and the path she takes is much longer than the stories of Miguel and Luisa, because Susan Stires (2002), then a staff developer and researcher in Alice's school, accompanied Alice from pre-K through her 5th-grade year, the year she came to the end of elementary school and stepped over to the path of a middle school. Here we briefly consider the first 3 years of her schooling, with a focus on 1st grade and the ways in which science content appears and reappears.

Alice: A Quiet Pre-Kindergartner

In pre-K some of Alice's classmates are fluent in both Cantonese and English by the spring of the year, even though they start the year speaking only Cantonese. In contrast some children like Alice, who are considered to be "quiet," are just beginning to use English in a range of activities. Like the children we described in the Head Start rooms, those in Alice's room are allowed to speak the language(s) of their choice and given opportunities to engage in play of various kinds, including dramatic play. And adults' respectful acceptance of each child's style of participating—or not—was an important commonality in the Head Start and Alice's rooms, separated though they are by time and space. Details of Alice's pre-K year appear elsewhere (Stires & Genishi, 2008); here we illustrate how her language and literacy knowledge changes over time while her interest in science and social relationships persist.

We begin with an example from pre-K. In a lengthy group discussion of a book about butterflies that you encountered in Chapter 2, Donna Yung-Chan describes how the caterpillar is growing bigger and will turn into a butterfly. Children chime in enthusiastically.

After Ms. Yung resumes reading the book, Alice says something first in Cantonese, then: "Ms. Yung! (gesturing with her hands to indicate *small*) Small, still small. Baby!" Alice comments on her own observation and later has a sidebar conversation with James in Cantonese, occasionally using the word *butterfly*, animatedly pointing to the book. Thus other children verbalize more than Alice, some in combinations of Cantonese and English, but she is clearly immersed in science via a book, in learning about how caterpillars become butterflies. The process is even more gripping because of the butterfly box in the pre-K room, where several live caterpillars are demonstrating the process. This attraction to living things is nurtured by Alice's future teachers who continue to weave the content of science and social studies into the conversations of EBs and into their early literacy learning.

Science, Language, and Relationships: Alice's Literacy Learning in a 1st-Grade Context

According to Susan, in kindergarten Alice is emerging as a bilingual; she uses English in the public arena of the classroom when participating in lessons, but Cantonese with her friends and tablemates. At the end of the year when writing what she has learned in kindergarten, she writes that she learned "the English," progressing far beyond the English of her pre-K year.

In 1st grade, Alice's spoken English is fluent and still developing. Like other children from her pre-K class, she is working through the grammar of English. For example, note the structure of the following sentences, as her 1st-grade teacher, Rosie Young, and the children discuss how to tell whether a baby chick is male or female. Alice seems to have been reflecting on the problem:

> *Alice* (to Ms. Young and the class): I have something else. Hum, then when the chick come out (of the egg), and when the chicks are big, and then the one chick have eggs, then you know a girl or boy. (Stires & Genishi, 2008, p. 64)

Not all of Alice's grammatical structures are conventional since, for example, she does not yet have the rules for creating certain kinds of complex sentences: "Then you know [whether it is] a girl or boy." This is not surprising as researchers have found that rules like these develop over a period of years in first-language learners as well (C. Chomsky, 1969; Karmiloff-Smith, 1986). Yet the ideas are clear: You can watch chicks until they mature; then you will know which are female since only "girl" chickens lay eggs. A long-term solution, perhaps not efficient—but a logical one! And Alice shows a scientist's confidence in follow-through and observation.

We highlight this example because it reflects how Alice's language learning interweaves with her fascination with science and her relationship with peers and her teacher Ms. Young. In the 1st grade she socializes around her reading. Even for her expert projects on bears and chickens, she works with her friend Matthew, also Chinese American and learning English. In guided reading groups (Fountas & Pinnell, 1996), where her teacher Ms. Young is always present, Alice enjoys making observations and discussing them without the backdrop of science content.

She makes predictions and connections with the text, along with inferences as she empathizes with the characters. One day in a discussion of the differences between Arnold Lobel's characters, Frog and Toad, Alice makes this announcement:

Alice: I'm like Frog.
Ms. Young: You don't like to stay in bed (like Toad)?
Alice: I don't, I don't, I don't. I love to get up. In the morning I'm
    hungry. And when I finish my breakfast and then I tell my dad to
    wake up and go to work. And then he always be late for work (pause)
    faster. (Stires & Genishi, 2008, p. 57)

Alice routinely and energetically answers Ms. Young's questions about the stories they read.

By the end of the year Alice is reading fluently and expressively, although she is hesitant to decode unknown words. So even if she knows part of a word, or rime, like "eat" in "treat" or "owl" in "growl," she is unable to blend it with the onset. In writing, however, Alice is much more adventurous. There is a core of words that she can spell conventionally, and she uses invented spelling liberally for the words she can't spell. Unlike reading, writing appears to be more like play for Alice. She attends to Ms. Young's lessons, but Alice also chooses what to attend to, often writing letters, stories, or lists that are independent of lessons. Thus writing becomes a habit for Alice by the end of 1st grade.

Alice's engagement with science continues throughout her elementary years. Indeed by the 5th grade she has joined an after-school science club and tells Susan that science is her favorite subject. Alice has the unusual good fortune of having Ms. Young as her teacher again in 3rd grade. They are still in touch with each other, and Ms. Young is still one of Alice's favorite people, a teaching companion for 2 years of elementary school and a friend in the years following.

Following Alice: What Have We Learned?

The distinctive path that Alice follows from being a quiet pre-kindergartner to a confident 1st grader is instructive from multiple viewpoints. She shares with Luisa what appears to be a watchful attitude. Thus her inner clock is different from that of children like Tommy, whose inner clock runs fast. In the 1st grade her English syntax was a bit "different" from that of some of her peers, but she is able to communicate her complex ideas in English to her teacher and friends. Alice, too, illustrates most clearly the influence of specific content, that of science in her case, to motivate communication first privately in Cantonese, then publicly in English in both small and large groups.

As the years go by, Alice, Luisa, and Miguel cease being EBs (emergent bilinguals), as their bilingualism has flowered. They are heard to use both their Spanish and English (Luisa and Miguel) and Cantonese and English (Alice) in the classroom. Yet Alice uses Cantonese less and less, raising the question of when she is no longer an EB or even "bilingual" in the school context. The issue of "language loss" is one that is a real-world companion to discussions of bilingualism and bilingual education but is beyond the scope of this chapter. For now we consider how time served as a companion to the language-learning processes of the five children featured in this chapter.

LEARNING LANGUAGES IN DIVERSE TIMES

As the artist Georgia O'Keeffe noted, no one takes the time either to see a flower or, she implies, to have a friend. Following the stories of Alice, Luisa, and Miguel, we would amend that observation to say that hardly anyone takes the time to see children, the small flowers in this era of accountability, to allow time for friendships to develop, or to understand how much time children need to learn everything on offer in classrooms. The teachers of these five children do indeed see the children as young learners and allow the time that leads to the languages of friendship and schooling, embedded in play and other curricular activities in their respective classrooms. Alice's story that extends to the 1st grade shows how language and literacy are later embedded in all aspects of the curriculum. Her language about science, both spoken and written, demonstrated the growing complexity of her ideas and her abilities to express herself in English.

Time Is of the Essence

The sociolinguistic progress made by all the children in this chapter—Pierre, Tommy, Luisa, Miguel, and Alice—happens in part because their watchful and active teachers create a flexible curriculum in which they encourage the use of nonverbal and verbal language and can see when individual "interventions" are needed. For instance, Luisa's teachers are able to suggest to her parents that she have a hearing test.

The progress also occurs over time—a long time. Miguel and Luisa appear to adults in the 3s and 4s classrooms to be extremely quiet children for more than a year; Alice is just beginning to speak English at the end of pre-K, her 1st year in school. Yet all three children show themselves eventually to be not only *emergent* bilinguals, but *actual* bilinguals.

Moreover, Miguel and Luisa are becoming biliterate in Spanish and English, whereas Alice is becoming a reader and writer of English. The three are active learners who appear to be "on grade level" in subsequent years of schooling. Yet in terms of becoming speakers in the classroom their inner clocks run against the norm of "most children" in our highly verbal society. They follow their own distinctive paths to the common outcomes of using language(s) in speech and print.

This happy confluence of child agency and learning and flexible teaching philosophies is unfortunately seen in few schools. Especially for children labeled "at risk" in schools where families have relatively low incomes, it is more common to see a focus on reading skills and scripted curricula. In turn educators' and policy makers' sense of time has become distorted: time is compressed so that "one schedule fits all." Thus, schedules are not adjusted for children's individual tempos, and school time is marked by tests and end-of-year events like promotion or retention. (We will discuss policy makers' sense of time further in Chapter 6.)

Further, the dominance of computers has created a sociocultural clock that is ever faster, resulting in a "psychology of hurriedness" (Gleick, 1999, p. 9). Events that cannot be activated and ended by a click or via remote control are perceived as slow. From this perspective, the time that it takes to experience unhurried events is conflated with wasted time.

The psychology of hurriedness bears a resemblance to another theoretical view of time, that of "panoptical time," which "emphasizes the endings toward which youth are to progress and places individual adolescents [or children] into a sociocultural narrative that demands 'mastery'"(Lesko, 2001, p. 107). Panoptical time captures in a compressed way children's learning, defined simplistically as "mastery," or satisfactory test scores. Indeed, a synonym for panoptical time could be "NCLB time," with its fixation on Adequate Yearly Progress, measured by standardized test scores. Test scores next to a list of children's names—such a stark contrast with the lifelike anecdotes of Figure 3.1—demonstrate a particular kind of mastery of skills and incorporate only the narrow objectives of prescribed curricula.

There is nothing in test scores that captures the social aspects of the curricula that the EBs in this chapter respond to and gradually weave into their own life narratives in and out of school. And test scores would certainly not capture their pleasure and nonverbal and verbal excitement, their words tripping over the words of others as they try to articulate their eagerness to play and to learn.

Within the context of panoptical or NCLB time, the notion of a child's inner clock may seem either romantic or misguided—anachronistic, so to speak. Children's understanding of time, after all, is supposed to be underdeveloped (Piaget, 1969/2007). Given that little is known about children's sense of time, however, we could hypothesize that children are like adults, who behave as if the norm is to have variable inner clocks (Barkley, Koplowitz, Anderson, & McMurray, 1997; Yamamoto, 1979).

As evidence of this variability, note the essentializing representations of entire cultures that are said to share a particular norm regarding time. For example, social psychologist Robert Levine (1997) recounts his experiences teaching in Brazil, where he found that lateness for class and social engagements was not only tolerated, it was expected. By contrast, he describes the Japanese to be both punctual and nearly phobic about wasting time or passing time that is not devoted to work. Thus, time is of the essence in disparate ways across cultures, and of course in any culture, individuals follow or resist the supposed norm.

Multitemporality: Teachers' Sense of Diverse Times

To bridge divergent interpretations of time, Levine (1997) introduces the concept of *multitemporality* as an ability of individuals to adapt to different conceptions of time—that is, to move quickly when speed is required and to slow down when the pressure is off. This seems akin to *code-switching,* or alternating between dialects or languages depending on the person addressed or other aspects of a situation (Blom & Gumperz, 1986). The flexible teacher may indeed have learned to be a multitemporal "time-switcher" when taking the perspective of a roomful of children, each with her or his own inner clock.

Each child's inner clock is metaphorically set for the time it takes to live an individual life—the time it takes for Tommy or Pierre to go from action to language-and-action or for Alice, Luisa, or Miguel to go from quietness to fluency. These children's diverse language stories unfolded in relatively unhurried time. Everything that happened to them—their arrival in their pre-K rooms, the good fortune of being in classrooms with attentive adults—happened in the relatively unpressured time of pre-K. So did all the morning meetings in Ms. Yung's room and meals in Head Start, when teachers said repeatedly in Spanish and English, "What do you say?" to teach the modest social skill of showing gratitude with a "thank you" or "*gracias.*"

There are millions of children like Pierre, Tommy, Luisa, Miguel, and Alice who will take a little or a lot of time to learn another language. Researchers say that learners need 5 to 7 years to learn academic discourse (Cummins, 1979, 2000). For all language learners time is of the essence, but not in the legal sense—where whatever is named in a case *must* happen within a short time. That would be NCLB time. Unhurried time—the time it takes to learn to express yourself—is of the essence as well. Like the teacher in *First Grade Takes a Test,* we know that children need that time to show what they are *able* to do.

Recall that one day in her Head Start 4s room, Luisa's friend Josué says, "Someone stop. Luisa wants to play." And Luisa answers with high energy, "I play, I play!" proclaiming to all her readiness to participate verbally. What a reasonable desire for a pre-kindergartner, and what a sensible path to offer in classrooms for young children if we want EBs to enhance their sociolinguistic flexibility in varied contexts that are worth talking about. The ways in which playful contexts continue to be central in children's lives are the topics of the following chapter.

4. Play, Story, and the Imagination

N. Scott Momaday has imagined a dialogue between Bear and Yahweh in his book *In the Bear's House* (1999, p. 40). In that dialogue, Bear asks Yahweh,

> Language. How did it happen? How did language begin? Yahweh answers,
>
>> Oh, the children made it one day.
>> Poor Man, he had been trying so hard to talk for such a long time. Then the children went out and played together. At the end of the day, they had possession of language.
>
> Yahweh tells Bear that the children came home, saying to their parents,
>
>> "This is what you have been trying to say."
>
> To which Bear replies,
>
>> Language is child's play.
>
> Yahweh affirms,
>
>> There you have it.

Then the children went out to play, the story goes, and language was its essence. The core of this story is apparent whenever children gather to play in an imagined world. To get the fantasy going, and to sustain it, children rely in large part on language. To take their roles and make their dramatic moves, children may manipulate not only their words but their very voices—their intonation, volume, rhythm, and pitch—and so become a bad guy, a superhero, a mommy, a baby, a kitty. Moreover, children learn to attune to one another, to collaboratively take their turns and tie their meanings together in some kind of narrative sense: Pretend it's nighttime, it's morning, it's time to go here or there or maybe to bed. In these ways, children become social players in worlds they jointly make.

Thus, fantasy play can be, as early childhood teacher Vivian Paley (2004) illustrates so well, "a nourishing habitat for cognitive, narrative, and social connectivity" (p. 8). For our purposes here, it is a setting that, for children, may promote communication and language use and, for teachers, may provide a window into children's interests and concerns, their beliefs about human relationships and, moreover, their ways of using language to take a social role. What could be a better "habitat" for language learning than play? What could better promote the sociolinguistic flexibility we aim for as educators of the young? And what could potentially allow teachers a better view of the language and social lives of children?

It is surprising, then, that play, this ancient tool for language learning, is at risk in contemporary early childhood classrooms. Imaginative worlds, especially those story worlds enacted in play, are being squeezed out of young children's classrooms. Indeed, from the vantage point of the current early childhood scene, Miriam Cohen's test-taking 1st grade is no doubt much more fictional than she could have imagined in the book's first edition (1980). Not only are the dated clothes missing from the new edition (2006), but so are the dolls, along with the toy vehicles and the playhouses on the now books-only shelves. These toys index child play, and that too is on the shelf, struggling even to hold on in classrooms for younger children.

Columnists for the *New York Times* (e.g., Brody, 2007; Williams & Feldman, 2007), along with the American Academy of Pediatrics (October 2006), have bemoaned the highly structured after-school lives of children. Middle-class children's lives are frequently dominated by special classes listed on crowded family calendars. The classes are to further children's competitive advantage in intellectual pursuits, artistic creativity, and athletic prowess (Lareau, 2003). But, say the pediatricians, unstructured play is the time-honored avenue for creativity, social relations, and problem-identifying and -solving.

Still, our concern is the nature of young children's lives inside classrooms, where the accountability movement has engendered a sense of urgency—of no time to waste—and, thus, a rush to get those playful children in line and on the road to reading test achievement. This is no mean feat, given that children have their unique rhythms, tempos, and volume levels; their varying home languages and styles of communication; their particular interests and dispositions; not to mention a predilection to play. And while this affects all children it particularly influences the education of those at the center of NCLB's concerns: low-income and minority children (Kantor & Lowe, 2006).

Of course, we have tried to get the children in narrow lines before. There have long been concerns about children who are so-called at risk—the majority of children in many of our urban and rural schools—and about the time these children may spend playing. In the 1960s, for example, Bereiter and Engelmann (1966), in their compensatory program for preschoolers who were so categorized, assumed that play and story were fine for economically advantaged children, but "disadvantaged" ones could not afford to have curricular time "devoted to play. . . . [If it were, poor children] might acquire whatever it is that middle class children get out of their extensive occupation with these things. . . ." But, "whatever it is" would take time away from academic learning (p. 12).

The labels may have changed from "disadvantaged" to "at risk" but the belief still holds. Truth be told, though, it is not so easy to ban play and story from classrooms. As children sit together, even in the most regulated of classrooms, they may play all manner of games, as long as they are subtle about it. Using mainly their voices as a means for play, children can become a "fake" family, complete with roles for sisters, brothers, moms, and kids; then there are owners and pets, girl friends and boy friends, professional athletes, and radio-singing stars (e.g., see Dyson, 2003, 2007). Along with these dramatic personas, told stories, plays on language, and child-invented jokes may slide into open spaces.

Still, what do children gain—and what might we as educators gain—from allowing play and story to have an official place, particularly in a normal classroom of linguistically and culturally diverse children? This is the question we consider in this chapter. We first feature preschoolers just learning Spanish or English and then 1st graders who speak African American Language (AAL). By illustrating the complexity of children's playful interactions with peers and teachers, we aim to paint rich portraits of childhoods, children's resources, and "whatever it is" they get out of play.

IMAGINATIVE PLAY AS A MEANS
FOR LEARNING LANGUAGE . . . AND VICE VERSA

In play, said the Russian psychologist Vygotsky (1978, p. 102), young children are at their "highest level" of development. And this, he argued, is because playing children deliberately and willfully guide their actions by meaning, not just by the literal qualities of their surroundings.

That is, to play together children construct imaginary situations in which meanings and perceptions have a "mediated" relationship (Franklin, 1983; Vygotsky, 1978, p. 103). Objects and people can be reimagined and renamed as something other than their literal selves. For example, a small child can become a giant monster, a mad mama, or a hip radio star; a scrap of paper can become a menu, a speeding ticket, or marked with skull-and-crossbones, a treasure—it all depends on the intentions of the playing children.

Language is clearly important for this renaming, but so are other kinds of resources. Among them are children's own capacity for movement and coordinated action, relationships that are familiar and responsive, and shared experiential knowledge, including the characters, plots, and themes of both everyday life and the popular media (Garvey, 1990). Despite the importance of shared experiences, playing children do not follow a script. Rather, as the childhood sociologist Corsaro (2003) details, children orchestrate their manipulations of objects, voices, and, indeed, languages themselves as they repeat and extend one another's contributions to the making of a world. Play, then, is a socially complex communicative act.

The improvised but experientially grounded play was evident, for example, in how Amy, just 23 months, interacted with her "baby" and her mother, trying to get her mom to act properly motherly, as it were (Miller, 1982; see Chapter 2). It was evident as well in how 6-year-old Lyron and Ezekial negotiated the language of "tough" dudes with "mean" cars (see Chapter 2). And it is evident in the two examples below from the Head Start program for 4-year-olds we visited in Chapter 3. As we explained earlier, Luisa, whose heritage language is Mixteco, is just learning Spanish, then English; she can be seen at the periphery and then in the center of playful goings-on. Through these examples, Luisa and her peers demonstrate the mutually supportive relationship between language learning and play.

Luisa at the Edges: Pretend It's a Birthday

One day, when Celia was visiting, Sarine, an English speaker, became a director in action and word of a communal event, a birthday party. This was a pretend party, since no one in the room was having a birthday on this day. And it was a party that could only have happened within a group that had shared a social and imaginative history, even though the children did not always share a common language.

Part of that social and imaginative history was the use of plastic fruit and vegetables from the family/kitchen area. Those plastic objects had a lot of symbolic "currency," mainly as gifts for friends but also as pretend food or, sometimes, as commodities for playing store. In addition to those designated presents, Sarine had reliable fellow partygoers—her good friends Melissa and Tina. All three girls shared English, although Tina was bilingual and Sarine spoke a little Spanish. But they also shared with many children in the room, whatever their language proficiency, some knowledge of birthday parties.

The party began when Sarine noticed Celia sitting taking notes and decided to reimagine or rename Celia as her "oldest cousin" and the recipient of a present, a plastic food present. Melissa followed suit, repeating her friend's action, and then present-giving escalated, as many objects from different parts of the room were piled, bonfire style, on a blue tablecloth from the kitchen/family space, now lying in the block area. All the plastic vegetables and fruits quickly ended up in the pile, and then, within minutes pots and pans, dress-up clothes, and more, topped off with dress-up butterfly wings, were added.

Soon, caught up in the flow of the party, children were arranging chairs in a semicircle in the block area. The chairs were for party guests. The children eventually put a hat and scarves on Dominga, the assistant teacher and newly designated birthday girl.

The head teacher, Ann, now called out "*No mas!* No more. Nothing else," pleading firmly but not angrily. The birthday party, though, had one last ritual—Dominga led the group in singing *Las Mañanitas,* the happy birthday song in Mexico (and in the classroom). Then came the activity that closes many lively play events: Children had to put all the presents back in their literal, real-world places. Still Dominga was a grateful guest. "OK, thank you very much," she said in English. "I'm so happy."

With classroom materials piled on the rug and the assistant teacher adorned with scarves, it was literally a bit of a mess. To see its organizational sense as a birthday party, one would have to observe the children as they coordinated their efforts, paying attention to one another, aided by their group understanding of the symbolic potential of plastic food and the rituals associated with birthdays. And one would have to appreciate their history as a group, most of whom were together as 3-year-olds. So the time spent together, their ensuing friendships, their sense of fun shared with teachers (until that point of *"No más"*)—all supported this lively child-led improvisation. One was hardly aware that the children spoke different languages, as they clearly understood the language and accompanying actions of "birthday."

Dominga, as teacher, was responsive to the child players' incorporation of her into their play. She used both Spanish and English to extend the play and build on what the children were doing. She even responded as a grateful guest; although, in the end, her presents had to be put back. Ann's role in the play was more subtle, but clearly she allowed time and space for play, observed its unfolding, and made decisions about what was "enough" in terms of children's movement of themselves and objects in the confined space of a classroom.

Like Dominga and Ann, adults in classroom contexts observe children's play, make decisions about when to join in and strategically interact with the players, suggesting a plot development, a role for a child wanting into the play, or writing down themes and issues for later discussion (Garvey, 1990; Paley, 2004; Van Hoorn, Nourot, Scales, & Alward, 2006). Across cultural and socioeconomic circumstance, adults assume different roles in relation to child play (Lancy, 2007). In school contexts, observant teachers can provide time, space, and considered support for children's interactions within the "meta-message"—the mutually understood laughter, dramatic voices, or spontaneous moves—that signals "This is play" (Bateson, 1956).

In Dominga and Ann's room, while the birthday party was going on, not all children chose to go to the party, of course. For her part, Luisa was close by but on the margins of the celebration. Instead she played with puzzles, a favorite activity at the time. In fact, her initial way of playing in the 4s room was with table toys, objects with (for her) literal and not imaginative functions: puzzles, dominoes, foam numbers that she did not recognize but that she arranged in the way that she wanted.

Luisa Enters In: Pretend It's "*Mucha* Raining"

Six months later, Luisa had entered into imaginative play. She had been surrounded by all kinds of play since entering the classroom. And she had been aided by ear surgery, which seemed to contribute to her becoming more talkative. She was becoming a more active dramatic player as well, using actions and words to create dramas and, sometimes, even to play with languages themselves. Indeed she could direct the play, as on the day "when it was '*mucha* raining.'"

Luisa was in her "house": the book area, which was a small square, with three "walls" and an open side that Luisa transformed into a wall with a door: she repeatedly locked the imaginary door with two locks. She seemed to be locking herself in, safe from the rain falling only in her imagination.

That locked "door," transformed by Luisa's actions, was apparently invisible to her friend Rebeca, who kept walking through it. Luisa adapted to her friend's actions and dropped the locked-door play. The inside of her house became the outside and the rain was named, allowing the girls to coordinate their actions more easily and thus enabling their play to become more collaborative. Although Luisa and Rebeca usually spoke Spanish to each other, Luisa seemed to instigate play with languages themselves:

> *Luisa: Está mucho* raining!
> *Rebeca:* It's raining.
> *Together: Mucho* raining! *Mucho* raining!

The two girls shriek "*mucho* raining," which becomes "*mucha* raining," as they chant for several minutes. Later they take out the eensy weensy spider puzzle, which does have "*mucho*" rain washing the spider out, as readers probably recall.

> *Luisa: Está mucha* raining.
> *Rebeca* (sings): The eensy weensy spider went up. . . .

In the context of play, the once-quiet Luisa displayed her interactional and linguistic skills. A few months earlier, Luisa's spoken language did not seem to be extensive enough to enact an imaginary drama or to play with Spanish and English words. But in the above example, Luisa used talk to engage her friend in her imagined rainstorm, and she also played with languages. (She had been heard earlier saying "*Está lluviendo*" ["It's raining"; the conventional way of saying "It's raining a lot" is *"Está lluviendo mucho"*].) Given the girls' intense enthusiasm, they seemed to be willfully and playfully code-switching in a fun-filled duet.

Luisa and her peers illustrate the cultural universal of play as a means for entering into a shared social life with other children. To build that shared life, children appropriate from and play with everyday stuff, including language itself. But to do so, they require time, space, interactional partners, engaging objects, and observant teachers who both further and document the communicative strengths revealed and nurtured by play.

In the section below, we highlight one aspect of play that becomes more prominent as children gain experience as language users and as players—children's dependence on language itself, rather than objects and their properties, to carry on their play. We focus particularly on the voices children may appropriate as they assume varied roles in imaginative play. This play with voices supports and dramatically reveals children's sociolinguistic flexibility.

PLAY WITH AND THROUGH VOICES: COMMUNICATIVE FLEXIBILITY

In the following vignette, 5-year-old Reeny is dictating to her teacher, Vivian Paley (1997):

> "Once there was a little princess . . . And a mother and father. They was the king and queen."
>
> "Do you want to say 'They *were* the king and queen'?" (asks Mrs. Paley.)
>
> "They *is* the king and queen." She hurries on lest I interrupt again.
>
> "And the princess was walking in the forest deeply and she got lost."
>
> *"In the forest deeply is nice,"* I offer, to which Reeny says:
>
> "Thank you. . . . Then the princess sees the opening and there is a prince."
>
> "And he says, 'Hi baby'?" Bruce snickers.
>
> "Uh-uh," Reeny replies with great dignity, "'cause, see, a prince don't talk that way. He say, 'Good morning, madam. How is Your Highness today?'"
>
> (Reeny) knows what a prince says and what boys and girls should say—and sometimes even what a teacher might refrain from saying. (pp. 3–4)

Reeny had a wealth of experiences with play and with stories read, told, and enacted. She knew how to negotiate identities with others and how to orchestrate voices to make a world, as Bakhtin (1981) would say. Based on that experience, Bruce's "Hi baby" was just not right for a prince. Bruce, in fact, had been greeting

Reeny herself that way, trying, perhaps, to assume the voice of a cool dude greeting a girl. But Reeny told him that that greeting was for his girlfriend. "And I'm not your girlfriend."

Reeny's use of talk to create a social scene—and her ability to talk about the situational appropriateness of talk—illustrates the sort of communicative flexibility that can be revealed and furthered, not only by telling stories, but also by enacting them in play. In making a "pretend" world, children sort out needed identities. Although these identities tend to be stereotypical, they allow children to negotiate dramas more easily (Garvey, 1990). For example, Mamas need babies, superheroes need bad guys, boyfriends need (willing) girlfriends.

To enact these roles, children may appropriate the language that typifies that role, that is, the generic "voice" (Bakhtin, 1981). Particularly for experienced players, appropriating that voice may entail varied kinds of linguistic adjustments. For young children, those adjustments might involve deliberate changes of prosody, like volume, pitch, and duration of sounds (Anderson, 1990; Garvey, 1984). Becoming a baby, for example, may entail raising the pitch of one's voice. A victim needing saving may yell "HE:LP," stretching out the word as it's spoken. And a teacher, or a mother, may sound quite firm indeed, as Tionna and her friends will soon illustrate.

Part of being a communicator is also knowing what to talk about when (Hymes, 1972), and decisions about vocabulary and topic matter in play, too. One does not, as Reeny noted, say "Hi, baby" in just any situation. Moreover, deliberate changes in sentence syntax or in ways of arranging words can be important for play, but for young players, such changes are sophisticated. Still, sometimes word arrangement is salient, because it is so intertwined with the enactment of a role. Listen, for example, to Mrs. Kay's 1st graders; Janette speaks, while Tionna and Elisha have their heads bent over small chalkboards.

> "Ready?" says Janette. "One time only. Train. I rode on a train before." Janette speaks in a clear, firm, authoritative voice. "Barbie. I play with my Barbies." (This is conversationally odd—a one-word sentence followed by another containing that word but unconnected to any ongoing conversation; it can only mean one thing: a spelling test.)
>
> "Tionna, come here," Janette soon orders. And Tionna brings her chalkboard up for Janette's inspection.

In playing school, Janette was clearly the teacher. Like whoever played that role, she used a teacher's authoritarian voice, issuing straightforward directives and adopting the discursively distinctive wording of a spelling test; moreover, she spoke in a formal way, with a relatively even pitch and careful enunciation of each word. A speaker of AAL, she slipped into a more informal mode only when Tionna demanded a score of 100%, something she would never do of Mrs. Kay. "That [paper] ain't no hundred percent!" Janette replied and, besides, she wasn't sure how to make 100%.

In playing school and other kinds of imaginative games, ways of talking, including choices of languages themselves, are potential resources for establishing roles and for moving in and out of those roles (Romaine, 1984). Thus, play provides contexts in which particular kinds of talk make sense. The demands, for example, of telephone play—with its imagined distanced partner (Gillen, 2002)—differ from that of, say, mom and baby-with-immediate-needs (*"Wa-ah!"*).

Observing children enacting varying roles and assuming diverse identities may reveal their communicative flexibility. To illustrate, we bring back to center stage 6-year-old Tionna, who, like Reeny, made no situated sense of her teacher's grammatical corrections (see Chapter 2). But also like Reeny, she was highly sensitive to how to manipulate language to play out roles. In the first section below, Tionna dramatizes her ways of slipping into varied voices by manipulating and stretching her language resources. In the second, she and her peers incorporate written texts into their play and enact their own version of "birthday" play; this play, though, unlike that occurring in Luisa's class, will remain outside the teacher's purview.

Samples of Tionna's Repertoire: Playing with Voices

In the unofficial or child-governed time and space of "inside" recess (or "activity" time), Tionna's play captured some of the diverse voices of her everyday life. She and her friends have already been portrayed as they played "school"; in that play, the "teacher" appropriated the diction, vocabulary, and interactional structure of a lesson. In contrast, children appropriated not the formal diction of official authority but the hip sound of stylish girls when they sang a radio song or enacted one of their many rhythmic "plays." Those plays have been particularly but not exclusively associated with African American children (Beresin, 1995; Gilmore, 1985; Jones & Hawes, 1972). In the following example, Tionna and her close friends Mandisa and Janette coordinate their words and actions to a rhythmic beat as (in quiet but distinctive voices) they play with family stereotypes:

> *Tionna:* We haven't done Boom Chicka in a long time.
> *Mandisa:* Let's do it.
> *Tionna:* Let's do it.

And Tionna, Mandisa, and Janette all clap and rhythmically say:

> *All:* (clapping) Bat man//On the train
> *Janette:* Watch these girls.
> *Mandisa:* Watch *them* girls. (correcting Janette)

> *Janette:* Watch them girls.
> *Mandisa:* Do their thing.
> *Tionna:* Do *that* thing. (correcting Mandisa)
> *All:* (clapping) Boom chicka// boom chicka boom chicka
>   Do it like your ma:ma.
>   Boom chicka //my hai:r (elbows bent, hands framing hair)
>   Boom chicka //my hai:r//Boom chicka //my hai:r
>   Do it like your daddy.
>   Boom chicka //my ca:r (rhythmically steering invisible car)
>   Boom chicka //my ca:r//Boom chicka//my ca:r
>   Do it like your sister.
>   Boom chicka//my nai:ls—
> *Tionna:* No, that's your auntie!
> *Mandisa & Janette:* OK.
> *Tionna:* Your sister go like, you know. (rhythmically moves hips)
> *Mandisa:* OK.
> *All:* Do it like your sister. Boom chicka boom chicka (move
>   their hips)

And on the girls go through family members young and old, male and female.

While it cannot be known how deliberate the children were in using "non-standard" features (e.g., moving from "these girls" to "them girls"), they regularly corrected words and rhythms in such language plays. As befitting a performative mode (Bauman, 1992), in this context, they attended to language's diverse material qualities—its rhythm and rhyme, its varied and manipulable sounds. And they coordinated their verbal and nonverbal actions, sometimes taking turns, sometimes in unison.

These plays were seen as girl affairs (and particularly Black girl affairs) but watched with admiration by many children. Mrs. Kay responded to her children's interest in rhyme and song by introducing those she knew to the class. Some she recited from memory and others she read from what became highly popular classroom books. Although Mrs. Kay's rhymes (e.g., the "Teddy Bear turn around" jump-rope chant) did not contain the dramatic enactments of the children's plays, she was joined enthusiastically by her children. Such songs and language plays (including nursery rhymes) are recognized as avenues for metalinguistic awareness of language's material or "sound" qualities (e.g., Bryant, Bradley, MacLean, & Crossland, 1989); but they are also avenues for enactments of dramatic personae.

Both the hip-sounding (and swaying) rhythm of "Boom chicka" plays and the formal, directive beat of playing school differed from the fast-paced but casually polite tone of "fast-food play." During activity time, Mandisa cooked Play-Doh patties while Tionna managed the counter. In exchanges with customers, the counter clerk managed the interaction, much as the teacher did in playing school, but the clerk sought "real" (if pretend) information and responded with goods as well as words, trying to keep "you" the customer satisfied:

> Miss, you want a drink to go with that (Number 10 burger)? Any sauce? Yeah? . . . Here you go. Have a nice day.

Tionna had the litany of questions, and the perfunctory "Have a nice day" down pat. Such a patterned ritual would not do for this final oral example, the improvisational turn Tionna took as Lyron's loving but firm "Mom" in Lego play. She was often Lyron's "girlfriend," and so she had to work hard to be his mom. When he resisted her narrative line (and her directives), she adapted, providing explanations and staying in charge:

> It is classroom activity time. Mrs. Kay is meeting individually with children to correct an assignment, and Tionna has chosen to play with Legos, as has Lyron. She tries to gain control of her house as "Mom" and to designate Lyron as her "son."

> > *Tionna:* Oh! I need these doors to go (here) . . . This is my small room 'cause I got parts to my house. Soon as you walk in there's a part right there—
> > *Lyron:* My picture's on the wall, when you walk in. (Lyron seems to be playing "boyfriend and girlfriends," but Tionna, at least for a little while, is trying out another role.)
> > *Tionna:* Yeah, this is *my* room, and this is my living room. . . .
> > *Lyron:* Where's *my* room?
> > *Tionna:* I don't know. I'll build it somewhere.
> > . . .
> > *Ezekial:* Can I play?
> > *Lyron:* Yeah.
> > *Tionna:* My room is *my privacy.*
> > *Lyron:* My room is *my privacy.*

Tionna and Lyron are tying their turns together, semantically (via word choices) and syntactically (via parallel word arrangement). Lyron has expectations for special treatment (his picture on the wall, a room of his own), but Tionna seems more concerned about her "privacy." Soon she adopts the directorial role of mother, deeming Lyron her "son"; Ezekial's access to the house is dependent on that "son."

> *Tionna:* (to Ezekial) You can live with Lyron and you can be in a
> room with Lyron and (his) junk.
> . . .
> *Lyron:* (to Ezekial): You gotta live with me. Tionna doesn't want
> you in her room.
> *Ezekial:* OK. I will.
> *Tionna:* Only my son can come in . . . You (Ezekial) can only
> come in if Lyron bring you in. I gotta take you to *school*
> tomorrow.
> . . .
> *Lyron:* I go to college.
> . . .
> *Ezekial:* Me and Lyron go to college.
> *Tionna:* I'm outta college. I already went to college. Y'all better
> not come in my room. Lyron you know it. . . . Only if I say you
> could. Son.
> . . .
> *Tionna:* (to Ezekial) Here's some water for you Ezekial. . . . 'Cause
> I don't want you in my kitchen. Only if my son comes . . . Or
> if you don't feel like getting up you could get that water. (To
> Lyron:) I gave him a bottle of water.
> *Ezekial:* Oh! I get a bottle! And your older son gets more. (Ezekial
> seems to think he's a son too, but Tionna sets him straight.
> Lyron does not need a bottle of water because he can come in
> the kitchen if he's thirsty.)
> *Tionna:* . . . My *son* gets to come in my kitchen! (To Lyron:) If
> if you bring Ezekial, he can—he—if you all go in my kitchen
> with Lyron I don't care. But don't let them go in the kitchen by
> themselves. 'Cause you don't know what they be doing.
> *Lyron:* OK. OK, Mom.

And with that "OK, Mom," Tionna had successfully negotiated her role (although, before long, she became the girlfriend who would marry Lyron, but that's another story).

Negotiating with her "son" and his friend necessitated reasoning within the parameters of her role in the play (i.e., being in charge of her house) and, as a mediator, using syntactically complex speech: Tionna explained that one could do this or that if, and only if, certain conditions applied, and these conditions mattered for such and such reasons. Just like she could appropriate with apparent ease the chants of the girls doing their thing, the queries of the fast-food clerk, and the directives of the teacher in charge, Tionna could appropriate a voice that sounded like it could be her own grandmother (her "mom"). One can almost hear her elder's voice in Tionna's "You don't know what they be doing."

One could view Tionna's talk against the "basics" list for 1st grade and decide that she and her friends were not measuring up—they were not talking "correctly" ("You don't know what they be doing" [see Chapter 2]). But one could also look at their talk in the contexts of their play and marvel at their ear for language and their communicative flexibility. Tionna and her friends were adapting their language to particular roles and circumstances—and this is what we want to foster for all young children, particularly those becoming multilingual and bidialectal. Indeed, as will be illustrated (particularly in Chapter 5), Tionna's playful propensity to appropriate situated voices, a propensity shared to varied extent with all children (Nelson, 1996), was a major resource for story composing and even for assuming the formal "standard" voice of her teacher's prose.

In our examples in this chapter, we have highlighted play as a communicative event, in which social experience is disassembled into roles and actions and then assembled as an "as-if-it-were-true" event (Goldman, 1998). Observers of child play have sometimes commented that the play of low-income children like Tionna and her peers, relative to those designated as middle class, is a more realistic appropriation of the adult world (e.g., Corsaro, 2003; see discussion, Andersen, 1990). It may be hard, though, to know what is a more "realistic" appropriation. Having a room of one's own, going to college, and even inviting friends to an actual birthday party can be a matter of imagination, not a close reproduction of reality. Our point is that any child's world is interwoven with a diversity of voices in and out of school and those situated voices provide resources for play. Thus, one potential outcome of play is much practice as a communicator in varied roles and situations.

Unofficial Play in Official Space: Pretend It's a Party

In Luisa's class, the children shared a social and imaginative history and this allowed them to generate playful communal events, like the birthday party described earlier. This was true in Tionna's room as well. More so than Luisa's teacher, though, Tionna's teacher was under pressure to concentrate on literacy "basics" (see Chapter 2). There was no time and space specifically for dramatic play, although, as just illustrated, the children did play.

In addition to inside and outside recess, the daily writing period was a prime time for play. As Mrs. Kay circulated or met one-on-one for editing conferences, the children stayed at their seats with paper, pencils, and each other. Educators have long described how simple literacy tools like pencils and pads are useful props for some kinds of dramatic play: for example, making grocery lists in "kitchens," taking orders in "restaurants," jotting down telephone messages, and even map-making for superheroes who are off to right the world's wrongs (Marsh, 1999; Roskos & Christie, 2001).

In Mrs. Kay's room, though, the children themselves generated a number of communal activities that transformed their individual writing tasks to communal play activities. One interwoven network of activities was generated by the planning of pretend birthday parties. Perhaps in response to Mrs. Kay's modeled writing of her plans for fun times, the children wrote their own plans; one popular form of such plans was a declaration about who in the class would be coming to their private birthday parties, even though the parties were not actually held (Dyson, 2007). These plans were variations of "This named child and that one and that other one are coming to my birthday." The planning of (pretend) parties recruited children from across the class, as children could gain an "invitation" to a party by promising an invitation back. And because children exerted pressure on tablemates to include them in their parties, party-goers crossed the usual friendship lines reinforced by gender and race. All of the children knew of the concept of inviting others to birthday parties; indeed, it was a part of local popular culture because of a much-advertised local fast-food place catering to child birthday parties.

The writing of party plans became a key practice in a network of unofficial practices that took place in—and outside of—writing time. The play required not only a birthday party giver and guests, but also a range of interconnected practices. These included making lists of potential invitees (and crossing out children from lists for one reason or another), oral negotiating about being invited or about who would be picking up whom, making invitations, and exchanging bits of phone numbers and addresses. To illustrate, Tionna herself reported on the practice of making lists of birthday invitees during inside recess (see Figure 4.1). And below are exemplars of oral and written invitations, all enacted during inside recess:

Ezekial has a pad of paper and a pencil for jotting down invitees and their phone numbers; he is moving around the room stopping to talk to this person and that one, and he now comes upon Joshua, who is playing with the Legos:

> *Ezekial:* Joshua, do you want to come to my party?
> *Joshua:* Party?
> *Ezekial:* Yep.
> *Joshua:* Yippee! I'll be there. (Note how there is no questioning
>   about date or time, no need to talk to parents; one is always
>   free to go to a pretend party.)
> *Ezekial:* 'Cause I'm going to (a fast-food place catering to
>   children) so we can play basketball there.

FIGURE 4.1. Tionna's Reported Birthday "lisiss" Play.

Me and J   and M
were Plaxiing lisiss to go
to areberday on Sunday 22
2002 and M   's
derday ison Wedsday 22'
and T   'sderdayisonthurs

Elly, witnessing the action, offers Ezekial a written invitation—and a polite request—to the current form of her anticipated party (a trip to California):

Ezekial   Plese
            come
            to
            Califony

Ezekial's big grin suggests that he is enormously pleased to be invited. (First presented in Dyson, 2007, p. 126.)

These interconnected practices provided communicative options for children seeking to enter and sustain birthday party play. The children's generation of these options was not so much a quality of a child's language use (like Tionna's illustrated flexibility) as a dynamic outcome of agency in a culture of children. Children eagerly participated in the birthday practices in part because they wanted to be named, to be included. If the curriculum had allowed for observation of that play, the children's interests and communicative events might have informed official efforts. Even the official classroom birthday parties, held for each child, could have entailed planning, composing invitations to special guests, and making birthday cards. And certainly there were critical issues to be discussed, without denying the children their play, chief among them the ethics of reading about private parties in public places (i.e., during classroom time for sharing writing) when some children were left out.

This is just one example of how playing children may appropriate from official and unofficial worlds in making an imagined world—in this case, one where fun events are always right around the corner. From Luisa's Head Start peers (and cooperative coteacher) implicitly analyzing and reconstructing a birthday party—its social relations, valued objects, and rituals—to Tionna and her 1st-grade peers' playful planning, children have illustrated how play may bring them together across language and sociocultural differences and, at the same time, serve as a context for language generation. In all cases, children have been enacting narratives, stories of what might be. In the final section we focus directly on the stories children compose in any medium.

TELLING STORIES:
CONSTRUCTING SELVES AND OTHERS THROUGH LANGUAGE

At age 3, Celia's nephew Chuck told a very short story:

Chuck puts two pieces of cereal together between his fingers.
"Sandwich," he says and then laughs. (First presented in Almy & Genishi, 1979, p. 132).

Chuck's laughter suggested that he knew that he was playfully entering the world of conversation and story: He became a little boy who made a (pretend) sandwich. Although stories are sometimes referred to as "monologues," they are always part of an ongoing human dialogue (Bakhtin, 1981). That is, a story comes out of a situation in which someone wants to communicate with someone else for some reason.

Telling stories, like enacting them, begins early in a child's life, with simple but meaning-filled utterances. These utterances may remark on the canonical—on what usually happens—or, more commonly, narrate the remarkable, the unexpected (Ochs & Capps, 2001). Through such language acts, children begin to tell, and to imagine, the story of themselves in the world (Miller & Goodnow, 1995). And, as Chuck also suggests, there is in fact a potentially close link between dramatizing an imaginary situation—playing—and performing a story (Vygotsky, 1978; Wolfson, 1982).

Listening to young children's talk may reveal this dynamic continuum between telling a story and performing or playing it out. That is, the border between telling and enacting stories can be quite tenuous. Consider, for example, 5-year-old Bryan's story—his "pretending"—in the vignette below. Within the situational constraints of classroom composing time, Bryan is both telling a story and playfully enacting it.

Bryan's teacher Mrs. Bee has asked her kindergartners to get with a partner and write words that might help them compose a personal experience story. Like other schoolteachers serving low-income children, she is under pressure to have a structured literacy program for her kindergartners. Still, Bryan and his partner DeShawn have transformed their "note-taking" activity (for generating words for their text) into collaborative storytelling. When Anne sits down beside him, Bryan tells her that he is "pretending" he is a basketball player, and then turns back to DeShawn:

> Bryan: I'm picking basketball (to play, not baseball like you). Like if you got the *ball*, and you *stole* it from somebody—
> DeShawn: . . . If you had the basketball and you hide it and say "I don't got it," and it was behind you, and you shoot it and, you know, get it off—that would have been tight, wouldn't it? Wouldn't it?
> Bryan: Yeah. And guess what? I'm gonna—I'm gonna—I'm gonna throw it up and then catch the ball, and then I'm gonna dribble it under my legs and then I'm gonna—and then I'm gonna do it again, and then I'm gonna throw it to the top (unclear), and then I'm gonna *dunk* the ball, and then throw it up at the rim, and do it again. (As Bryan tells the story of what he will do, he acts out his throwing, dribbling, and dunking.)
> DeShawn: Like Michael Jordan could do that. He could dunk with one hand. He could dunk with one hand.
> Bryan: And then my team gonna win.

At his seat, Bryan draws himself making his moves and then writes, acting out each sentence: I DKt It (I dunked it) I ShD IT (I shoot it) IPtu My Lz (I put it under my legs.)

In Chapter 5, we will examine the importance of play and drawing in young children's written language; here, though, it is the storytelling itself that is of interest and, in particular, its link to play and language. Bryan was *into* basketball. He was not using his time to "take notes" but rather to "pretend" through narrating with his friend DeShawn. In his storytelling, Bryan appropriates the discourse of an important part of his world ("dribbling," "dunking," and that all-important "rim") to become the master of the ball, his dunks leading his team to victory.

Although Bryan is participating in a "literacy" event, his storytelling is appropriated from a particular kind of narrative event—one found on a basketball court, not in the covers of a book; and the storytelling act itself is supported by the familiar collaborative structure of play. Bryan thus suggests that there are many kinds of narratives that children may use to locate themselves in, and construct, their worlds.

However, in school, "good" stories and "literate" ones tend to be tied to a dominant Western literacy tradition. This tradition does not include the diversity of children's storytelling, not to mention the variably structured and multimedia nature of many children's favorite texts, including not only audiovisual productions (e.g., sports shows, movies) but also beloved picture books. In Tionna's 1st grade, her teacher Mrs. Kay followed the mandated curriculum guides; in these guides, a story is to have a linear sequence—a beginning, middle, and end; a fictional story (one in which one "pretends," in Bryan's words) requires a central problem and motivated characters who work toward a solution. While this is an important kind of story, there are others that matter, too. What, for instance, is the "problem/solution" in the habitual action of *Brown Bear, Brown Bear* (Martin, 1983) or the descriptive detail of Cisneros's (1997) *Hairs/Pelitos*?

Although Mrs. Kay modeled personal narrative texts with linear structures during composing time, throughout the schoolday she made space for and responded to varied kinds of storytelling. For example, she allowed time every morning for children who had "something to tell us." This morning time allowed Mrs. Kay to learn about her children's lives outside of school, and it also provided children with opportunities for extended language use. Moreover, storytelling supported Mrs. Kay's efforts to build relationships among the culturally and racially diverse children in her room, and thereby form a classroom community. Below, we will listen a while to Mrs. Kay and her children tell their stories.

The Social and Language Possibilities of Group Storytelling: "This Is What Happened to Me"

One morning much like many others, Mrs. Kay's children sat on the rug, raised their hands, and one by one told "what happened." Mrs. Kay, for her part, responded as one might to a conversational narrative, providing evaluative remarks or asking questions to promote a fuller story. Elly, usually full of elaborate stories, today reported quite succinctly that her dad was having his hip replaced. Mrs. Kay asked for the where and the when and then said:

> You know what, Elly? I'm so happy for him because he's been in a lot of pain, hasn't he, with that hip? So that's awesome. Now are you going to be able to go visit him? (Elly shakes her head.) Oh, not 'till he comes home.

Mrs. Kay thus learns something important about Elly's family, something that may account for her more subdued nature on this day. Aaron also has had a significant event—his dad, who works outdoors, has returned to work. As she did for Elly, Mrs. Kay provides key contextual information (i.e., the weather has warmed) and evaluative commentary (i.e., that's good but he is probably tired). Mandisa, like Jon, has a story that features her uncle. Her story is performative: She replays her dialogue with her uncle with gusto, her intermittent giggles anticipating her peers' laughter:

> *Mandisa:* Yesterday . . . me and my mom went to the store and um when she was there, she saw um my uncle Robert. I call him Uncle Boo. (We) went over there for Labor Day and . . . Uncle Boo was saying, "Go home," and I was saying, "I don't want to go home" (giggles).
> *Mrs. Kay* (laughing along with class): He sounds like he's kind of a teaser uncle. Does he tease you a lot?

Soon comes a story about an anticipated move (a common theme) and, also, a string of stories about watching videos, usually for the umpteenth time. These stories tend to generate a buzz among the children, as they attest to having seen, or planning to see, the show, too, or playfully revoice what they regard as funny dialogue. One such story is Ezekial's—although, as is usual with him, he works one of his big brothers into the narrative:

> *Ezekial:* I'm watching *Like Mike*. And I watch it a lot. . . . When I was watching last night, my brother Joseph he said Janette called me.
> *Mrs. Kay:* Oh yeah? So Janette called you last night.
> *Janette:* Yeah, but my cousin took the phone.
> *Mrs. Kay:* Oh. (sympathetically) So you didn't get to have a conversation.

Finally, Tionna tells a story that brings together the moving theme with that of relatives. Tionna, as Mrs. Kay knew, was not moving and, indeed, did not move for the 3 years Anne kept in touch with Mrs. Kay and her children.

> *Tionna:* When I move my um my grandma says she will buy me a swing set and she will ask my uncle if she can bring my baby cousin down there so I can have somebody to play with. And she says she will probably.
> And she says when we move she's gonna make a garden 'cause there's a place where you can make a garden.
> And she says when we move we will live by my Uncle Tina and when we move I can go to my uncle's house.

Mrs. Kay, concerned about the accuracy of Tionna's story, responds with, "Are you *sure* you're gonna move?"

> *Tionna:* She said this summer.
> *Mrs. Kay:* She said she thinks this summer. Ah.
> *Tionna:* We'll take our beds too, 'cause last time when we moved we slept on the couch.

Mrs. Kay's children told stories that varied in purpose, in structure, and in the support needed from Mrs. Kay in this situation if their story was to be fleshed out. Consistent with the curricular benchmarks, Mrs. Kay viewed her role as, in part, helping children learn to tell detailed personal narratives. And yet, children seemed to bring many purposes, and many kinds of story structures, to group occasions for storytelling.

Sometimes the goal was indeed to share specific information about an event. But, on other occasions, it was simply social affiliation, some version of "I am going to see that video, too." Since the video was widely known, and the goal was to affiliate with those who had seen it, there was no need to provide details on the film (cf., Dyson, 1993). Another common purpose was performance and, more particularly, to make children laugh, like Mandisa with her story of Uncle Boo. Those stories could be exaggerations of what happened, often centering on something funny someone said.

Mrs. Kay, like all teachers, seemed on occasion to be on a different wavelength than her children. For example, Tionna seemed to be imagining a hypothetical and much desired future event, one she may well have discussed with her grandmother. This was a familiar tack for Tionna, reporting something that made her life full of pleasures just-around-the-corner. The story is poetic, with its repetitive references to what her grandma said; it is not so hard to imagine it as a picture book on, say, a dream home. Still, Mrs. Kay valued truth-telling, the detailed facts, and in this she sometimes seemed frustrated, like on the day that she told of her own plan to stay in a motel on a weekend trip and then, lo and behold, many children in the class were going to stay in a motel on the weekend—or, at least, were going to imagine themselves as doing so.

What accounts for these differences in storytelling? Are some children just "better"—more detailed, more truthful—storytellers than others? What factors matter in why, how, and what children tell as story composers?

The Interplay of Culture, Situation, and Individual Style in Storytelling: "Guess What?"

Children's ways of telling stories are learned through observing and partici-pating in narrative practices in their families and, as they grow older, in schools and peer groups, and in the wider popular culture (see Chapter 2). For this rea-son, cultural differences may be found in, for example, ways of getting others involved in one's story or of arranging narrated events; there are even differences in the criteria for judging a story as worth telling (Ochs & Capps, 2001). None-theless, children do not have only one way of telling a story; communicative situ-ation, including purpose, matters in what and how a story is told.

For example, during sharing times in Mrs. Kay's room, the children did not tend to tell stories centered around some problem needing to be solved. But one day the student teacher Ms. Hache told a story about solving the problem of her car not starting after school on an icy-cold day. The children responded with their own stories about being in some particular place with some particular family member needing to get somewhere when the car would not start, and they also told how they (or rather, a caregiver) solved the problem.

Individual variation in storytelling works against making simple, direct links between a child's cultural heritage(s) and a narrative style (Hester, 1996). Still, young children come to our classrooms with different kinds of narra-tive repertoires informed by various cultural traditions. For example, African American traditions include highly performative narratives, often improvisa-tions on experience. Mandisa's narrative about her uncle, and her retelling of the teasing dialogue, is illustrative. Stories in this tradition may seem rambling to "mainstream" ears, as they sometimes thematically link events separated in time and space (Cazden, 2001; Michaels, 1981; Smitherman, 1977). The lengthy story Tionna told Anne about her baby cousin, excerpted below, in-corporates such linking:

> *Tionna:* And he (my brother) was just teasing my baby cousin. And I—And
> I pushed him, 'cause he was teasing my baby cousin. My mom said

> whoever mess with my baby cousin I gotta—I gotta hit 'em. They can't
> mess with my baby cousin. They can't even slap my baby cousin with
> me being around. 'Cause she's only eight months.
> *Anne:* Oh my. Eight months. Too little to stick up for herself, huh?
> *Tionna:* When my mom's around, my mama, she be having—she be
> having a extension cord. She always have a extension cord. Whoever
> be messing with my baby cousin she'll whoop them. She whoop me if I
> mess with her too. But I don't mess with my baby cousin.
>
> When she get bigger, I'm gonna play with her. I do play with her
> when she's little too. I teach her how to walk. I hold her hand. And I ().
> She be going a slow walk, and I go fast. And last time I let her go, and
> she fell. And she was crying. And I had to hold her.

And on Tionna went to more episodes about her baby cousin who sometimes "get on my nerves" but whom she defends against others.

The unfolding of actions seemed less important to Tionna's peer Ezekial. He could tell elaborate fictional tales when drawing and, like many children, he enjoyed retelling the funny parts of a movie. Nonetheless, he often told Mrs. Kay brief stories that at least mentioned his big brothers. Mrs. Kay said she found his stories hard to respond to because they centered on people she did not know. She wanted to flesh out events with their who's, where's, and when's and to help provide evaluative commentary. Ezekial seemed to want to locate himself in important relationships. One day, after Mrs. Kay told what made her happy, Ezekial commented:

> *Ezekial:* One time my brother Manual called me a midget.
> *Mrs. Kay:* And that makes you unhappy?
> *Ezekial:* That makes me happy because he says he's just kidding
> with me.

Varied ways of telling stories provide rich resources for building relationships and for fostering language in oral and written modes. And certainly, as children gain experience in school, they may also gain appreciation of the fluency and the humor of an elaborate performance (Gallas, 1992), the feelings of connection undergirding a family story, and the reciprocal listening and talking possible when stories are brief and inviting. To aid in this process, parents and other community members can bring their own stories to tell in school, be those stories traditional tales, improvised performances, or personal narratives.

There are, of course, many more kinds of narratives than we have considered here. For example, Bryan's and DeShawn's storytelling was linked to broadcasters' moment-to-moment narrating of a sports game, which itself differs from newspaper reports, and it also recalled both film and book renditions of the athletic superhero Michael Jordan. And most American schoolchildren know about the multimedia stories called "movies," which interweave music, movement, and talk. Different children will have access to, and be involved by, varied modes and manners of stories. But, for all, stories will be the stuff through which they construct themselves as people with interesting histories, involving presents, and future possibilities in a world shared with others.

STORIES ENACTED AND TOLD:
THE LANGUAGE OF CHILDHOOD

Children are surrounded by narrative productions, and as we have emphasized, they appropriate and adapt those practices in their classroom lives with teachers and peers. Their stories may be enacted, told, drawn, and/or written, but they are always infused with the rhythms and melodies of their varying voices. Their play and stories belong not only in the unofficial world governed by children but also in the official world of language-rich and child-focused classrooms.

The classrooms in which we met Sarine, Luisa, Tionna, and Bryan were full of children learning from their teachers and from one another to use language to serve imaginative play and story—and of adults, including us, learning how play and story could stretch and enrich the language of children. As Yahweh told Bear, "Language is child's play" (Momaday, 1999, p. 40).

In listening to the language and play of children, teachers learn about their diverse experiences, interests, and concerns. Still, if children are observed in only one kind of play, or if their stories are heard through the filter of only one kind of narrative, then teachers' own professional stories of the children in their care will be underdeveloped. Teachers' stories should contain the nature and breadth of situations (e.g., topics, playmates, props) that entice individual children and thus reveal and further children's communicative roles and repertoire (including languages themselves). As they move both through and across time and space, children's language use ideally becomes both more linguistically fluent and situationally adaptive. As language and literacy educators, as teachers of the very young, it is this sociolinguistic flexibility, and children's sense of themselves as agents in a world of possibilities, that we aim for. Thus, through this chapter, we have worked toward returning time and space for play, story, and the imagination to a secure place on the curricular shelves.

5. Written Language in Childhoods

"Listen to me!" said the 1st-grade teacher in Miriam Cohen's (1980/2006, n.p.) story to her dispirited children, upset about the standardized test. The teacher wanted them to remember what they could do. Not only could they read books, but they could build things, like Jim and Paul's undersea racing car. They could make pictures! They had good ideas! And they could be helpful and kind to one another (when they did not have to shush for a test).

Since the initial debut of Cohen's book in 1980, though, young children's social and symbolic play in school has become expendable; there has been an institutional and political push for formal literacy instruction and testing (Bergen, 2006). And yet, as we will illustrate in this chapter on child composing, social relations and symbolic play are critical resources for written language learning, just as they are for speaking.

Indeed, throughout the preceding chapters, we have already seen children using these resources and, thereby, making composing "relevant" to their childhood lives, a quality Vygotsky deemed critical to learning to write (1978, p. 118). Kindergartner Bryan enacted a story with his friend DeShawn in which he became a basketball whiz like Michael Jordan; he then recontextualized—adapted—that play to his drawing and writing, thereby keeping the "pretend" identity intact. Luisa's peers in the pre-K used their organized dramatic actions and their appropriations of birthday rituals to "compose" through their actions a spontaneous story about a birthday party. During official writing time, Tionna and her 1st-grade peers wrote about pretend birthday parties, and that text-mediated play gave rise to a range of unofficial literacy practices (like making, and revising, lists of invitees). Tionna herself drew on her linguistic resources as she bragged to her friends in writing (and in talk) about getting a big present: "Is [It's] big."

All of these children were engaged not simply in individual acts of self-expression, but in kinds of communal activity. They were learning from their teachers about symbols and their use, but they were also using those symbols to

81

take action in childhood worlds. Their composing illustrates "the prehistory of writing" (Vygotsky, 1978, p. 105)—the way in which young children's use of the complex written symbol system builds on their experiences with other symbolic tools. This view of children as experienced makers of symbolic worlds provides a powerful lens for understanding young children's early entry into school literacy.

On the one hand, children's experiences with written language outside of school may vary greatly in nature and extent. This variation exists because language is infused with social and cultural meanings whatever its mode (oral, written, or some multimodal combination). Opportunities for, and ways of, using written language, like oral, are tied up with cultural, linguistic, and socioeconomic factors, along with personal interests and dispositions (Barton & Hamilton, 1998; Clay, 1998; Heath, 1983; Levinson, 2007; Street, 1993). Young children thus come to school with varied experiences with, and knowledge and know-how about, print.

On the other hand, all children bring their symbol-producing predilection to school—their talking, drawing, playing, storytelling, and, in our society, some kind of experience with print. The ability to share symbols and thereby organize and express inner feelings and experiences is a part of all children's human heritage. Familiar communicative practices, and comfortable symbolic tools, offer resources with which teachers and children can build new possibilities.

As will be evident, we are not opposed to the traditional "basics": We have no vendetta against the alphabet song, no discomfort with the rhymes and language plays that promote an awareness of language, no grudge against talking about letter sounds. We ourselves have engaged children in such activities, as do all the teachers we observed. But we know that, to use the words of Katherine Nelson (2007), precisely because children's previous experiences are so varied, what they learn from any encounter "cannot be prespecified or predetermined" (p. 258). Moreover, we also know that learning written language, like oral, is a social process; ways of making meaning through print are learned through participation in communicative events. The more constrained these events, the less likely it is that children can make their diverse resources relevant to the goings-on.

Thus, in this chapter, we feature children participating in events involving "tasks with scope" (Clay, 1998, p. 237; McNaughton, 2002)—that is, tasks that allow children to participate in different ways with different resources. Such tasks allow teachers to observe what children attend to and, so informed, to extend their knowledge and know-how (Love, Burns, & Buell, 2007). Among such tasks are drawing pictures, dictating stories, and engaging in varied kinds of official (teacher-governed) and unofficial (child-governed) writing activities.

Below, we first elaborate on the place of writing in children's symbolic repertoire and, second, consider the multiple dimensions of the dynamic medium of written language. We then illustrate the nonlinear route young children take as they attend to, are guided into, and take some social control over written language; we include in these illustrations attention to children's potential for communicative flexibility in this medium, a flexibility we have already highlighted in discussions of children's talk and play. We end by summarizing our themes and then considering the beliefs about childhoods and literacy that undergird trends toward scripted programs and mandated assessments for child writing. If we are not diligent, an appealing but challenging medium for many young children may become a medium for early school failure.

WRITING IN CHILDREN'S SYMBOLIC REPERTOIRES

"Many people assume a route from apparently meaningless 'scribbling' to recognizable depictions of recognizable objects" (Matthews, 1999, p. 5). Matthews was discussing drawing development; he was concerned that the activity accompanying and interwoven with children's drawing—their talk, actions, facial expressions, and movement between graphic representation on paper and other forms of symbol use (block building, dramatic play)—was deemed developmentally and aesthetically unimportant. But drawing develops within a repertoire of representational and expressive media. In using these symbolic media, children grapple with qualities like closure and boundaries, inside and out, linearity and rotation, movement and speed, rhythm and tempo; in the process, they learn both about these qualities and about the semiotic possibilities of varied media. Children's drawing is couched within and shaped by their interaction with paper and markers, with other forms of symbolic expression and, also, with appreciative, curious, or collaborating others.

Much the same could be said about children's writing (Dyson, 1989). It, too, is often portrayed along a linear line, from scribbles and mock writing to inventing spellings that map sounds onto written letters, leading ultimately to texts that are not only readable but also increasingly long and complex. But one problem with this linear line is that it hides from view the central role in literacy development of children's symbolic repertoire; within that repertoire, children find a niche for print.

Many years ago, Vygotsky (1978, 1987) helped explain the importance of children's symbolic repertoire to written language development. In his view, written language differs from oral language in the challenges it poses for children. In learning to talk, children spontaneously appropriate words used by other people. These meaning-saturated signs, born in dialogue (Bakhtin, 1981), are the basis for children's "inner speech"—that is, for their capacity to think with words. In learning to write, children have to deliberately reflect on and consciously choose signs that will help them represent and communicate their intentions. Young children more readily experience the deliberate manipulation of symbolic stuff in dramatic play and, then, in drawing, block building, and other means of constructing symbolic worlds. These experiences can support and augment their efforts to use, and to differentiate, the particular strengths of writing.

You might recall Reeny, a young student of Vivian Paley, who dictated a story about the princess "in the forest deeply." Paley has provided many examples of preschoolers and kindergartners like Reeny who are deeply engaged in dramatic play, and then draw on that play for the deliberative process of dictating stories. Their written narratives could then be transformed into informal theater, as Mrs. Paley read each dictation aloud so that children could listen to and infuse meaning into the read words by acting them out with and for their peers. In this way, their initial stories, enacted in play, were transformed and brought to dramatic life once again, at a slower pace and in a public situation where teacher and peers might offer new perspectives on the stories or question their meaning (e.g., the nature of princely talk; see Chapter 4).

Tionna was another eager composer, the author of previously cited texts about sharing popcorn, getting big presents, and preparing for pretend birthday parties. She also illustrates how children differentiate a niche for writing within a symbolic repertoire. Consider, for example, a provocative excerpt from a text she wrote during the daily writing period:

> We are going to play a
> wer (war) it will (be) the girls a gints the
> boys all the girls are going
> to bet the boys nobody can stop the girls because
> we have a 1,0000001500000 (a thousand hundred and fifty million) of
>   misssl and the boys
> oldy (only) have one missl no way
> the boys can bet the girls thay
> can't lay a (hand) on us no you cant
> stop us not a bit because they
> don't have a nofe things
> to get adit (attack) us we are tofe girls . . .
> (written by Tionna in May; first reported in Dyson, 2007, p. 129)

This text was not simply an individual expression of written meaning but a conversational turn in an organized, multimodal event. Tionna was participating in communal play that originated as the "Pine Cone Wars," a team chase game played during recess. When recontextualized to writing time, the game became a composing (more accurately, a drawing, talking, and writing) practice (Dyson, 2008b).

Like Tionna, the other players from the Pine Cone Wars used drawing to indicate how the team's home bases (their space castles) were positioned relative to one another; drawing, after all, lends itself more easily than writing to depictions of spatial relations (Kress, 2003). They also used drawing to indicate the direction and fast tempo of laser blasts, using angled, quickly drawn lines. All the while, they could call attention to their drawing and orally narrate their team's next moves, thereby keeping the dialogic play in motion. At Tionna's worktable, originally only boys were participating in this indoor textual play; their written pieces were quite brief (e.g., "Me and Manuel are going to have a war. I am going to winn. . . ."). As we will discuss later in this chapter, written texts became more elaborate when Tionna—a girl—entered her male peers' play and the conversational sparks began to fly over and then on the page.

Thus, the Pine Cone players composed events that were relevant to their childhoods—to the themes of their play, including the grappling with gender categories, the pleasures of power, and even the notion of "war." Their writing, rich with potential topics for classroom discussion (e.g., on "real" and "pretend" war, on gender and physical power), did not come simply from "scribbles" but from their experiences and ongoing engagement as social agents and participants in a range of symbolic practices involving worlds at once "make believe" and intensely real. Time to play, to draw, to talk, to hear stories and to tell their own across multiple media and technologies (Comber & Nixon, 2004; Jenkins, 2006; Marsh, 2005; Pahl, 2003)—these are means for helping young children recognize written language as a relevant tool for their lives.

Against this backdrop of young children as social players and symbol users, we now take a closer look at the complex written system and, then, at the diverse ways in which children may learn of its nature and functional relevance.

THE MULTIPLE DIMENSIONS OF WRITTEN LANGUAGE

Through varied means, and to differing extents, written language is on display and in use in children's worlds. They learn through participating in written language events: they observe, interact with knowledgeable others, and try using the system themselves. The use of this medium, though, has multiple, interwoven dimensions.

For example, we expect a language event, written as well as oral, to have some social purpose, a kind of message or content in a certain structure or order, and we note the writer's (or speaker's) tone or attitude (Hymes, 1972). In any society, there are typical events that call for typical kinds of texts or genres. As children observe and participate in these events, or literacy practices, they learn through talk (Heath, 1983); they hear and see texts as they are voiced by parents, teachers, popular figures, and community members. As children experience them, then, certain kinds of text quite literally have a typical voice (Bakhtin, 1981), a typical sound. The celebratory voice of the "Happy Birthday!" greeting card, for instance, is quite different from the monotone of the grocery list, the melodious sound emanating from the church hymnal, or the melodramatic dialogue of the superhero cartoon . . . or the sports media.

It is no wonder, then, that children may read and write messages even before they control the conventional symbol system. Moreover, their writing may be guided by voices from a range of human and technological sources, including ones familiar in classrooms (like children's literature) and ones from their everyday lives (e.g., sports figures, movie, television, book characters, and popular singers [Dyson, 2003]). Bryan, for example, could assume the voice of a basketball insider; he "dkt" [dunked] that basketball and, in his play, "dribbled it" under his legs, so that his team would win. Reeny, on the other hand, dictated a "once-there-was" story, appropriating typical features of a fairy-tale narrator; within that tale, a princely character spoke in a princely voice: "How is Your Highness today?" These appropriated voices can be tied to identities of varied sorts. For instance, Tionna's male tablemates felt that war games were the stuff of "men," not girls; hence the "tofe girls" entered not only into a local childhood practice but also a societal and ideological struggle. In a related way, bilingual children might code-switch between languages as they read and write, a potential means of deliberately playing with and displaying multilingual identities (Reyes, 2001).

Literacy events display not only how writing sounds, but also how it looks, its perceptual features (Clay, 1975; Levin & Bus, 2003). Writing, whatever the script, has a certain linearity, a particular directionality, and specific kinds of units and of arrangements in space. Children from an immigrant Chinese family, for example, or one from Syria or India may well encounter (and learn) scripts with strikingly different material features (Kenner, 2004). And just as children may compose messages with, for example, cursivelike wavy lines, they may draw what writing looks like without any particular message (Levin & Bus, 2003). In so drawing, they explore print's perceptual qualities in approximate and then more precise ways, sometimes sure that they have made writing that an older person could read even if they cannot (Clay, 1975).

From an adult perspective, children's written symbols may clearly differ from their drawn pictures, but both are graphic means of representing and communicating meaning. Those shared features may help explain why children who distinguish pictures from print in a book, for example, may still use the word "writing" to refer to the act of "drawing" (Dyson, 1982; Matthews, 1999; Statesenko, 1995). Adults sometimes slip from writing into drawing as well, trying to articulate some idea that's just beyond their grasp (Witte, 1992).

In the written language system, though, symbols do not directly link to referential meaning. Rather, its units—its arrangements of letters and spaces—are linked in a systematic way to *spoken* language. Thus, writers rely on some kind of encoding system as they make decisions about which and how many letters to use to represent spoken words.

In their first efforts to encode a message, children may make letters that directly represent, or belong to, a referent; an "A," for example, may belong to Ashley or Alicia. They may even choose letters based on the size of the referent (e.g., large objects get many letters; Ferreiro & Teberosky, 1982); more conventionally, they may base decisions on the number of syllables (Ferreiro & Teberosky, 1982) or the sound-related qualities of letter names (Read, 1975). With experience and feedback, children may "invent" more phonemically complete representations of consonant and vowel sounds (Read, 1975; Richgels, 2001; Scharer & Zutell, 2003). As Alicia will illustrate, the very same child may use a range of encoding strategies, depending on that child's purpose, the complexity of the message, and the ongoing situation.

These dimensions of written language are not parallel strands but dynamic, interwoven ones. Children orchestrate these dimensions, guided by their understandings of what it is they are trying to do. Those guiding intentions and practices may come from both the official world, governed by their teacher, and the unofficial one, organized by their peers. The children discussed in the next section illustrate how children's orchestration of their written language knowledge and know-how—that is, the processes through which they write—varies with regard to their experience and interests and, moreover, with an event's purpose, participants, and symbolic tools.

In sum, written language is a slippery, complex phenomenon. Its multiple dimensions are "kaleidoscopic" (Clay, 1998, p. 141), their nature shifting with the demands and possibilities of the communicative situation. Children have differing experiences with this system, but they all have experiences to bring to bear as social players and symbol users.

We illustrate these experiences in the following sections, as we bring on to our textual stage Tommy, Alicia, and Tionna. These children have different linguistic and cultural resources and different personal interests, not to mention different curricular situations. Still, they all use their diverse experiential resources to construct understandings of the complex symbolic and communicative tool of written language; and they use that tool to participate in their social worlds in new ways.

REMIXING RELEVANT RESOURCES:
THE WRITTEN MEDIUM AND CHILDHOOD WORLDS

> Tiny Tatie, not yet 3 years old, never says a word and never comes
> to circle where we read the names and talk a little about letters.
> I am amazed to discover that she has been walking around the
> classroom all morning with two fingers in the shape of a *T*. When
> asked what she's doing, she says, "It's me," and continues silently
> to parade her *T* around the classroom.
>
> —Cynthia Ballenger (1999, p. 45)

Cynthia Ballenger offers this observation of Tatie from her preschool classroom serving Haitian immigrant families. Tatie will help us set the stage for our own stories of Tommy, Alicia, and Tionna.

To begin, Tatie underscores children's need to make personally relevant the complex print-strewn landscape of school. Tatie had her *T*, and that *T* was "me." At the same time, she illustrates that these personally relevant texts, however tiny, can mediate children's relationships with others. Tatie announced herself to her classmates with her *T*. And when Suzanne's mother visited the class, Tatie "colored a huge *S*" for her (Ballenger, 1999, pp. 45–46). That S was a greeting, a kind of reaching out on the common ground of a perceived convention—particular letters belong to particular children.

Tatie's ways of writing were reductions of the complex written system, ways to make it manageable. For her, written language became symbols for people and, as such, she learned her letters. And yet, the writing was semiotically complex; that is, it involved multiple symbol systems. Tatie thus reminds us that child writing is all wound up with their use of other media. Tatie enacted her *T* and made a picture of Suzanne's *S*. That is, she used familiar symbolic tools to construct her entry into written language. At the same time, those other media helped her fulfill her intentions. The finger-formed T, the parade around the classroom—these declared her literate presence in a way that a lonely *T* on a paper could not.

In our staged stories of Tommy, Alicia, and Tionna, we will position a spotlight on these individual children, but those children will not be alone. Like Tatie and her *T*, their multimodal constructions will mediate their social connections to others. Our stage is constrained by our page limit (just as the children are by their curricular expectations), but it will be long enough to allow us to follow the children across tasks and events. In this way, we will be able to illustrate how children's ways of making writing relevant and manageable vary, along with their purposes, interactional partners, and available media.

And so we begin now by turning our spotlight on Tommy.

Tommy: Writing on the Street

Tommy, whom we met in Chapter 3, was a lively, energetic child in Donna Yung-Chan's pre-kindergarten class in New York City. Ms. Yung's class was not a designated bilingual class, but it was a classroom that offered a variety of hands-on activities that furthered children's talk. Among Donna's children, Tommy, a native Cantonese speaker, stood out in part because of his great interest in written language. That interest will be evident in the vignettes to follow; those vignettes are situated within the often playful, constructive activities Ms. Yung made available to her children.

When young children like Tommy (or Tatie) become engaged with literacy, their first stable graphic symbols tend to be related to their everyday worlds—to their names or those of family members, or oft-noted environmental print from home and neighborhood (e.g., *A* could be the letter of one's sibling or of one's apartment door). Ms. Yung took advantage of this, and of Tommy's interest in print; she probed his knowledge of sound-symbol connections and, in the process, also extended his oral and written language, not to mention his drawing:

> Tommy makes a picture of a "night" full of stars after his "reading" of *Goodnight Moon* (Brown & Hurd, 1947). He then starts drawing a tall building on his page. Ms. Yung notices this and asks Tommy about that building—his "apartment," she suggests. She helps him write parts of his apartment address on the picture: his apartment number, 9-D, and his street, MRDSN (Madison Street). She asks him, for homework, to find out the number of his apartment building.

The next day, Tommy did not seem to have done his homework, so to speak, but it was clear that he had thought about the print on his street. Without prompting from Ms. Yung, Tommy transformed his apartment picture into a 3-D construction in the block-building area. His tall-drawn building became one of a number of long, rectangular blocks, vertically positioned on the floor. Horizontally placed blocks became the now clearly represented Madison Street. His constructed world needed signs, and so he cut small pieces of paper, wrote on them, and then worked to tape them in their proper locations. Below Ms. Yung talks to him about his productions:

> *Ms. Yung:* Why don't you talk about all the signs that you have?
> *Tommy:* This one's 9-D. (pointing to a sign)
> *Ms. Yung:* Your house, yeah, and—
> *Tommy:* This one's STOP, 100, and—(pointing to varied signs)

Ms. Yung: Ten miles an hour, and what about—
Tommy: It's one hundred!
Ms. Yung: One hundred miles! That's too fast for cars, don't you think, Tommy? And what do you have there (pointing to those horizontal blocks)?
Tommy: Um, Madison Street.
Ms. Yung: Oh, that's good. So when people go down the street, they know where they're going now. Down Madison Street.
Tommy: Madison Street, New York. (first reported in Genishi, Yung-Chan, & Stires, 2000, p. 73)

Just as Matthews (1999) suggested in his discussion of children's drawing, Tommy transformed his initial interest in his building as he interacted with both his teacher and his chosen symbolic media. His informal lesson with Ms. Yung was woven into his self-initiated constructive play. Writing was a functional tool in that play; it was needed in his three-dimensional symbolic world, just as it was in his experienced world: writing provided necessary labels and important regulations for drivers, real or pretend. Tommy took the initiative, and his observant teacher was able to stretch his oral and his written language and, in the process, to learn about Tommy's experience of his city street, not to mention his growing interest in and abilities with print.

Tommy learned not only through interactions with his teacher but also through talk with peers. In the vignette below, Tommy envelopes his peers Jeffrey and Ashley in his free-flowing play. In that play, Tommy manipulates the sounds of language itself, displaying a kind of metalinguistic insight critical to literacy learning. Understanding the orthographic nature of the written system entails, at least in part, understanding that words are composed of manipulable sounds—in other words, developing phonemic awareness.

Against this backdrop, listen to Tommy, a new speaker of English, and his peers Ashley and Jeffrey, both also native speakers of Cantonese:

On the table are markers, paper, and a box of blocklike wooden stamps that have upper-case letters on them. At first the three children attend to the physical activity of stamping, but Tommy soon leads them into play with language itself:

Tommy: I wanna write something. A question mark! No, no, no, no, not that. . . .
Jeffrey: A question mark go like this. (motions with his hands)
Tommy: Dee-goo. (The first of many "baby-talk" words that he creates)
Ashley: Why you say dee-goo?

Tommy: (some further baby talk) How about this stamper?
Ashley: What's called?
Tommy: A stamper-stamper.
. . . (omitted talk)
Tommy: December! (to himself) I don't want D. How about this
    B? Pretty big B?
. . .
Tommy: Need a little one.

Tommy seems to be looking for a lower-case letter, as he is going to write his peer Brian's name. He doesn't find one. But he does use those upper-case stamps—on Ashley's paper!

Tommy: A stamper—I stamp yours! (stamps Ashley's paper and
    laughs) I stamp it! (followed by more playful back-and-forth of
    trying to stamp someone else's paper).
. . .
Celia: Did you stamp that? (to Ashley)
Ashley: Tommy.
Tommy: Sticky! I say sticky.
Ashley: Sticky.
Jeffrey: Tom said sticky.
Tommy: Not me! HE! (pointing to Ashley)
Ashley: He??
Tommy: No, not me. He, Stoo:ky!
. . .
Tommy: How you do that, Stooky-hole?
Ashley: Stooky-hole? How you say that?
Tommy: Jeffrey!
Jeffrey: Me?
Ashley: No, I say "Tommy."
Tommy: I didn't say that (stamps Ashley's paper again). Cool!
Ashley: Stop!
Tommy: That's is some music.
Ashley: Those word. What words? (She points at Tommy's paper.
    Tommy has written, not stamped, Brian.)
Tommy: "Brian." I'm giving to Ms. Cipriano (the assistant
    teacher).
. . .
Tommy: I'm gonna make a little more wacko—a gumball. This is
    a gumball. (Starts drawing something that looks like a gumball
    machine.)
Ashley: Did you say gumball?
Tommy: Jeffrey said.
Ashley: I don't call you Jeffrey.

> *Jeffrey:* Not me—is Tommy.
> *Tommy:* Not me—HE!!
> *Jeffrey:* (inaudible) You say me one more time, I'm gonna hurt
>   you. (Nobody is hurting anybody.)

In the midst of the back-and-forth banter, it is easy to lose sight of the oral and written language in play (literally) here. The children are collectively playing with, and examining, letters and "words" (or, at least, a word—*Brian*). And they are playing with oral language as well. There are interactional games of identity ("You say me one more time . . ."), and perhaps efforts to figure out what is nonsense and what isn't ("Stooky-hole?"). And then there is Tommy, playing with "stamper," "sticky," and "stooky," making nonsense words and evident rhymes ("Not me—HE!"). All the while, Tommy is stamping, writing, and drawing, slipping with ease among these media. In the end, the written word becomes a kind of present for his teacher.

Tommy, then, was finding manageable and relevant (not to mention fun) ways into literacy use. Guided by his teacher to write his address on a pictured building, he appropriated that labeling action and recontextualized it as writing signs for his 3-D city street. In the vignette with his peers, Tommy's production of another kind of sign, a name, was interwoven with a kind of playfulness that would not be likely to happen with his teacher but which, nonetheless, entailed all manner of literacy concepts (e.g., lower- and upper-case letters, words, and the deliberate manipulation of language).

Traditionally, the kind of metalinguistic awareness Tommy displayed was fostered in preschool, kindergarten, and beginning 1st grade, in part through oral rhymes, books with alliteration as well as rhymes, and varied sorts of games (e.g., card games in which children matched pictures beginning with the same sound). These were predecessors to phonics instruction (Strickland, 1998). Currently, though, phonics is emphasized in many kindergartens, as it was in 5-year-old Alicia's kindergarten, the child we bring on stage next.

Alicia: Writing Friends

Sitting by kindergartner Alicia, one would likely hear her tell her tablemates all manner of imaginative tales—how she saved her sister from a shark, for example, or how the bunny she saw "hopped so loud . . . the house jumped up and down!" But Mrs. Bee, her teacher, had little official time for listening to (or taking dictation from) Alicia's storytelling. Like Miguel's and Luisa's teachers (see Chapter 3), she and her students were under enormous pressure, because it was the kindergarten (not the 1st-grade) teachers who had to get the children reading and writing conventional texts by the end of the year. Mrs. Bee had recently moved to this midsized Midwestern district and to Alicia's school, which served almost entirely minority children from economically strapped homes. Like Ms. Yung, she had previously taught pre-K and was taken aback by the pressure and the daily provision of just 15–20 minutes of recess, the designated play period. Still, she liked the friendliness of the school, was familiar with most of the children's parents, and had ties to their small urban community through a local church.

Relative to Tommy, then, Alicia, who had not before attended a school, had a more structured literacy curriculum, with little opportunity for constructive and dramatic play. There was no consistent practice (e.g., dictation) within which Alicia's performative storytelling might readily serve as a literacy resource, nor was there any official public stage to channel her sociability. Nonetheless, like Tommy, Alicia, who spoke African American Language, negotiated relevant and meaningful ways to participate in writing events, as the examples below illustrate. Collectively considered, they show, once again, the productive interplay between interactions with teachers and with peers.

The district-paced writing curriculum was oriented around a daily writing workshop, in which children were to produce independently written texts based primarily on "real" personal experiences. By the winter months, drawing was to be relegated to a quick "sketch" to "plan" the writing, and writing was to entail encoding with "invented spellings" (Read, 1975), based on stretching out words and listening to their sounds.

Alicia was not marching to the beat of the paced curriculum, though; she was oriented toward drawing and was just beginning to make sense of the alphabetic system and of Mrs. Bee's lessons on letter sounds, stretching words, and manipulating letters. And there was indeed much for her to explore: whether drawing or writing, there were intriguing perceptual features—curves and angled lines, blank spaces and variously positioned dots; there were written symbols' potential meanings, including the ways that certain letters linked to her, her family, and her friends, especially her friend "Willo"; there was the question of how to encode messages longer than a name and how "stretching words" figured into this; and then there was the whole business of telling a "real" story through making pictures and letters, not to mention learning how composing was a way of interacting—even playing—with peers.

Alicia focused on different dimensions of the written system in different kinds of events. During the latter months of school, when she was interacting mainly with her peers and tablemates, Alicia wrote quick cursivelike waves or letters and letter-like forms; she would read her writing and that writing was often about her good friend Willo. Indeed, Willo finally told her to spell her name W-I-L-L-O, and Alicia did (after much feedback from Willo, including a practice session Willo organized on the magnetic letter board about her first and last name). *Willo* often stood out as a stable anchor in Alicia's sea of waves or parade of letters.

On the day in which Alicia produced the work shown in Figure 5. 1, she was influenced in part by the class's assigned task of writing a piece to their mothers in honor of Mother's Day. In clarifying the task for the children, Mrs. Bee had stressed that the children were to write to their mothers, not about their mothers. She dramatized with great comic force, as she explained that they should not say, "I love my mom," but perhaps, "I love you, Mom" or "You are the prettiest thing in my world, Mom." Or "If I could drive, I would buy you a car, Mom." The children laughed, enjoying Mrs. Bee's performance (even though many needed a little personal feedback to revise "I love my mom").

FIGURE 5.1. Alicia's Letter to Her Mom.

At her table, Alicia announced her intention to draw her family. Willo found a way to make a place for herself in Alicia's drawing:

Alicia: I'm gonna write (draw) my mommy and my dada.
Willo: I'm your sister.
Alicia: I can put you here with my mama and my dada.

Alicia did just that, and when I asked her to tell me about her picture, Willo piped up and explained, "We're playing sisters, on paper."

Then Alicia wrote. In her text, Alicia displayed an understanding of the perceptual features of writing—its directionality and linearity and the nature of its signs (although *D* and *P* slipped into each other, as did *I* and *1*); she even knew that a "fingerpoint" [a period] should end a line. (The name "fingerpoint" seemed related to Mrs. Bee's call for a "finger space" between "words.") Alicia repeated letters, including those from known names, and also the whole of Willo's first and last name (the latter has been removed from the figure). When Mrs. Bee asked her to read her writing, Alicia did so, framing her text as directed to her mother, just as was assigned:

Mom, you is me and Willo mommy.
I see Willo in my dreams.
Her is my best sister.

"Hey," Willo objected. "There's no two 'Willo.' 'Willo, Willo Willo,'" she said, reading her name in Alicia's text. That is, you should have read *Willo* more than twice (because there are more *Willo*'s in your text). But Alicia seemed to interpret Willo's comment as about her picture (i.e., there should not be two *Willo*'s). "No!" Alicia replied to Willo. "This you" (pointing to a figure in her picture).

In this event, as in most involving mainly interaction with peers, Alicia focused on producing writing that looked right and which fulfilled official requirements, as she understood them. At the same time, she had another purpose for graphic production, one emanating from the unofficial world—to play with and please her good friend Willo, who could serve as audience, critic, and collaborator. This unofficial purpose helped make relevant the official requirements and, indeed, entailed the essence of writing—anticipating, negotiating with, and answering others' responses by manipulating symbols. This purpose is more readily served by other children, whether through informal interaction, as in Alicia's case, or formal classroom sharing times (as in Mrs. Paley's dramatic enactments of texts). Moreover, the context of imaginative and collaborative play was a familiar frame within which Alicia could orchestrate at least some aspects of her knowledge and know-how for composing.

At times, Alicia's writing was more intently influenced by Mrs. Bee. Since there were 23 children in the class and Mrs. Bee wanted to attend to them all, she could not always interact in extended ways with Alicia. But when she did, Mrs. Bee focused her attention on encoding and provided interactional support for the complex metalinguistic process it entailed. Thus, Mrs. Bee and Alicia jointly participated in the official writing workshop practice and, in so doing, constructed a "zone of proximal development," to borrow Vygotksy's (1978, p. 84) term, within which they stretched Alicia's encoding. The nature of this zone changed over time, but, in the example to follow, Mrs. Bee was acting on her observation that Alicia had been responding more consistently to requests to match words and beginning letter sounds.

As the example will illustrate, "inventing spelling" involves more than a certain level of phonemic awareness and phonics knowledge. The inexperienced child writer slows down a stream of talk, textualizes some aspect of it, breaks it into words, stretches out those that are not known by heart, listens for their constitutive sounds, and relates those sounds to letters (which Alicia sometimes had to find on an alphabet chart so she could more accurately draw them); then the message has to be returned to time and again to remember what one is writing or to retrieve the next word in the message. Children who write relatively conventionally often routinize their writing in some way, repeating certain words or phrases from one text to the next and thereby reducing the difficulty. Alicia did that, too. With Mrs. Bee, she reduced her message and concentrated on encoding; in her texts, most people, pets, and things were "pretty."

In producing the piece shown in Figure 5.2, Alicia had begun by drawing her two cats, Tiger and Casey—a sophisticated drawing for Alicia. (Note the differentiated facial features and body parts.) When Mrs. Bee asked her what she was going to write, she responded "The cat is pretty." Mrs. Bee then helped her break down her sentence:

> *Mrs. Bee:* The, The
> *Alicia:* It start with D.
> *Mrs. Bee:* It's kind of tricky because it's two letters. You guys say "de," but it's—look at me, "the." (putting tongue between teeth)

In AAL, "the" is often pronounced "de." But these different pronunciations of "th" do not seem meaningful—that is, relevant—to Alicia; she seems at a loss as to how to respond. She is just beginning to grapple with the phonemic qualities of her own speech, so, relying on that speech, suggesting "d" indicates her emerging understanding. In the end, "the" is a word whose spelling will have to be remembered. Mrs. Bee tells her that that "tricky 'the'" starts like "truck" (which is accurate graphically, though not phonemically).

FIGURE 5.2. Alicia's Pretty Cats.

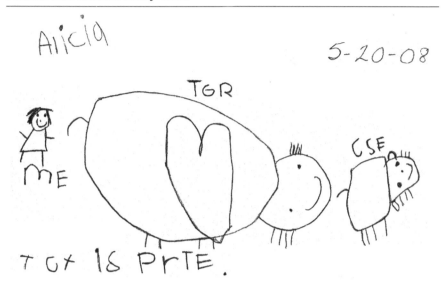

> *Alicia:* T like turtle? (looking at the alphabet chart, with its accompanying pictures)
> *Mrs. Bee:* Yeah. Why didn't I think of that? "The, cat." You need a finger space. . . . How do you spell cat?
> *Alicia:* C- T? (writes the letters)
> *Mrs. Bee:* A little T. "The cat" what?
> *Alicia:* "is"

And on Alicia and Mrs. Bee went, working their way through "The cat is pretty" and then rereading it, with Alicia pointing to each word. When they were done, Alicia had an idea for her picture.

> *Alicia:* I'm gonna put me right here. (Later she has the idea of a "heart" because "Cats have hearts, I know.")
> *Mrs. Bee:* . . . How do you write me? (Mrs. Bee is moving from a focus on representing "me" in the drawing to writing the word "me.")

And Mrs. Bee helps Alicia spell "me" and, eventually, the names of her cats, Tiger and Casey.

In her multimodal activity, Alicia leaned on other modes of representation, especially drawing, to represent her ideas. Her decision-making about her composition was most evident when she made decisions about the content of her drawing and, when she did so, Mrs. Bee learned something about Alicia's interests.

The last event sampled below illustrates the interplay of Alicia's interactions with Mrs. Bee in the official world and with her peers in the unofficial one. In this event, Alicia had decided to write about Dora, a popular television character and an animated Latina well known by all the children at her table. Alicia had been making letters for Dora, with no evident systematic encoding strategy. When I asked her what she was writing, she responded that "Dora is pretty" (her usual adult response). But Jamal, a tablemate, objected—C-H-I-W-I is not how you spell "pretty"! "It's P-E-T-Y," he said with conviction.

"That's not how you spell 'pretty,'" countered Alicia. And then, sometimes agreeing, sometimes disagreeing with her peers, Alicia, along with Anita and Jamal, sounded out (and shouted out suggestions for) the spelling. Alicia ended up with P [group concurrence], R [her own decision], E [at Jamal's insistence], and T [group concurrence]. She then quickly filled each line of her paper with CHIWIPRET.

Alicia's final text did not in and of itself signal progress, but the process did. She was not progressing in a linear line, moving from unconventional to conventional writing. Rather, she was participating in different literacy events, gathering different kinds of experience. If she viewed it as relevant and manageable, the knowledge and know-how thus gained could be recontextualized—adapted to the next event, always both familiar and new.

Through interacting with Mrs. Bee in the official world, Alicia was able to manage the complex encoding process in ways she could not on her own. In so doing, she routinized her message and thus reduced the difficulty of the process. Through interacting with peers in the unofficial world, Alicia was able to frame her writing within her social and playful relationships with others; she could manipulate her message to accomplish social work. In doing so, she routinized her encoding, so to speak, by repeating letters, names, and words. Thus, even in this relatively constrained curricular context, Alicia was able to negotiate a range of communicative events and thereby gain different kinds of experiences with the complex, multidimensional writing system.

As we leave Alicia (no doubt working out some matter with Willo), a final child is awaiting her turn on our stage. That seasoned performer is Tionna, a familiar character in our book, as is her hardworking teacher Mrs. Kay.

Tionna: Writing Voices

As you may recall, 6-year-old's Tionna's urban school was regulated by a mandated curriculum and by yearly standardized tests, beginning in kindergarten (see

Chapter 1). Her teacher Mrs. Kay had taught at the school for many years and kept certain long-standing 1st-grade practices—the morning meeting time when children could tell their stories, the activity time when children chose manipulative materials to play with, and if the weather allowed, twice daily breaks out on the playground.

To all these places, Tionna brought her out-of-school experiences and her language and, building on these, engaged in new experiences with teacher and peers. Like Tommy, she was intently interested in written language; she partici-pated in the daily writing time with evident eagerness (usually) and, like most of her peers, was audibly disappointed if there was no time for reading the day's texts to the class ("Ah, man"). Like Alicia, her official writing was often linked to unofficial relations and childhood practices. Indeed, from the beginning of the year, her journal entries included her friends Lyron, Janette, and Mandisa, and they included her. And, in time, communal childhood practices developed that enveloped them all (like the birthday party play described in Chapter 4).

What was most notable about Tionna's language use, both oral and writ-ten, was her alertness to the voices around her. This was evident in her play (see Chapter 4) and also became evident in her writing. Sometimes she adopted the conversational voice of her everyday storytelling; and when she did so, she used features of her AAL and, moreover, infused an evaluative tone into the rhythm of her written words—something even Mrs. Kay did not do in her modeled personal narratives. Just as she did in her oral stories, Tionna could use repeti-tions, comparisons, and direct speech along with explicit evaluation. The follow-ing piece was written during a period of consistent official reminders about a local happening for the school's families:

Today I am going to Impression 5 (a children's science museum)
my ant sue is going to take me
I hope she bring . . . Miah . . .
. . . (Miah) is my firs cusin
and the best cusint in the hole wide world
. . . I bet she will won't to do what I dow
she all ways copycat me
and I say aret you tier of copycatting me
she say no am (I'm) not/that is my favord
so plese stop ascking me mame (ma'am)
I get tier of that/calling me mame
so I will call her mame. . . . (slashes indicate additional line breaks)

Like Alicia, Tionna too did not seem to find relevant and meaningful her teachers' attention to her grammatical "errors" (e.g., "me and [somebody]," "peo-ple was . . .", "she say"), and she did not change them without explicit direction (as in the "i's" example in Chapter 2). Nonetheless, her ear for situated language—for the ways that people sound—seemed to account for how her language changed when she appropriated different voices, including that of her teacher. Her written dialogue with her cousin Miah was in the present tense ("she say"), assertive and, at least implicitly, back and forth. When she wrote her teacher's talk, it was more formal ("she said") and straightforward:

> Yesterday Mrs. Kay wint to the doctor she had to leav for the rest of the after non because she said her son Kelly had a bump on his arm she said they had to remove it.

Tionna's evident sociolinguistic flexibility was based on her attention to, and appropriation of, the rich voices around her in and out of school. And it marked her skill as a young writer, as much as did her spelling (based on sound, familiar visual patterns, and available word charts).

Tionna's writing curriculum, like Alicia's, stressed planned or reported true experiences (although the children often invented "true" experiences, as in the birthday play). But not only did Tionna incorporate voices into her personal experience stories; she appropriated new genres, new communicative situations, and these often grew out of, or became kinds of, unofficial peer play. This was possible because, as in Ms. Yung's curriculum, Mrs. Kay's allowed time for chosen activities with peers. And it was in that time that Tionna revealed the breadth of her written repertoire.

For example, one day Tionna's peer Mandisa was showing her and Lyron how to make "pop-up cards" for Mother's Day, a kind of card Mandisa's grandmother had taught her to make; that grandmother liked to make "arts and crafts" . . ."for the Holy Spirit." (In the children's conversations, their church was a major site for performative arts, including recitation, music, and arts and crafts.) Making pop-up books, then, was not a part of the official curriculum; it was a kind of knowledge and know-how that children brought to activity time and its ready provision of paper, scissors, and paste.

Tionna's card was for her grandmother (her mom). Following Mandisa's directions, she decided to decorate her card. She made a pop-up heart, traced a Barbie outline with a stencil and, then, remembered a poem she had read in her reading group that day. The poem read in part "Above the rest we think you are the best mom there could be." In her version of that poem, written in small letters on her card, Tionna preserved the formal tone, even using an archaic-sounding "be":

> Out of all the moms there be
> you are the best one
> there is in live.
> Happy mothers day love mom.

Despite that common confusion in her card (notice the "love mom," rather than "Love, Tionna"), she displayed once again an ear for a positioned voice. There was no avenue for the official use of this genre, although cards were commonly referenced genres among the children. Nonetheless, the pop-up, poetic card was formed through the interplay of Tionna's interactions with teacher and peers and of her involvement in official and unofficial worlds.

As already suggested, official writing itself gave rise to unofficial childhood practices, like those entailed in birthday party play. And, conversely, unofficial childhood practices could be recontextualized and adapted for official writing time. And this was the case for the Pine Cone Wars discussed earlier in this chapter.

When the boys at Tionna's table began to write about their war play, most of their communicative energy went into their drawing and talk. The boys had their own "teams" of many stick-figured men. The "teams" lived in "castles," and their battles unfolded in outer space. The medieval castles in outer space were a remix of varied images and plot lines from assorted cartoon series, as explained by Lyron (for more details, see Dyson, 2007, 2008b). Accompanying the drawing was talk, in which the boys warned one another what they would do or just did to the other's team. In contrast to the lively graphic play, the boys' texts were routinzed in content and structure, consisting mainly of statements of who would be playing whom in war and who would win. Their details of narrative action were not to be found in their texts—but when Tionna entered the play, the possibilities for written action changed.

On the day she began to play, Tionna had noticed that, at another table, her good friend Mandisa was planning her written war game, and so Tionna asked her if she could play, too. When Mandisa said "sure," Tionna began to draw the location of her space castle. Lyron, hearing her talk with Mandisa, objected:

> *Lyron:* Me and Manny have our own war. You guys (girls) don't even know about war.
> *Tionna:* Yes we do. I watched the war on TV.
> *Manny:* You're just copying offa us.
> *Tionna:* We got the girl war. No boys are allowed.

And now war play becomes gender play, another playground chase game. Jason, who sits at the table, gives verbal chase first, and Tionna refuses to play with him:

> *Jason:* (making weapon sound effects)
> *Tionna:* Jason, we're not playing in your war. We're not playing with you, in a war with you.
> *Jason:* You are.

Tionna: So you can kill us by yourself. You might be killing us, but we're
   not killing you and we're not on your team and we're not playing war
   with you guys. . . .
Jason: Okay.
Lyron: No! We're letting you guys (girls) play with us.
Jason: No man. A girl army's strong. (interaction first reported in full in
   Dyson, 2007, p. 133)

In Lyron's view, a girl was not eligible to play (or write) war. Tionna talked
back. Her good friend Lyron was not, at that moment, an invitee to her party, but
instead was a member of the gendered opposition. Tionna began her text with
the usual routine ("We are going to play a wer . . .") but she soon slipped into a
tough stance, literally talking back to the boys ("no you cant stop us not a bit . . .").
Tionna was not loving, like the author of the "all the moms there be" text; she was
authoritative, like a teacher or a mom, but aggressive, as befits a woman warrior. In
response, the boys also wrote more detailed texts, although, in their texts, the boys
won. Still, wrote Lyron, "The girls sed they will be back."

Mrs. Kay herself was unsettled by the gender war that erupted among her
children, and quite understandably, she banned war from that day on (a pedagogical action to which we will return). Nonetheless, Tionna's participation in
the Pine Cone Wars was yet another illustration of how children's multimodal
composing is shaped by their participation in official and unofficial worlds. In
this way, it echoes Tatie's T, Tommy's stamper play, and Alicia's *Willo*. More
particularly, it enriches the portrait of Tionna as a composer. She was an experienced writer who encoded relatively conventionally. Moreover, she was a
sociolinguistically aware composer: Her written texts varied depending on the
communicative situation and on the voices she was appropriating and making
her own.

As you may have noticed, her writing did not meet the "standards" as described in Chapter 1. Those "standards" included standardized English (as detailed in the kindergarten grammatical usage goals, all of which were to be evident
in 1st-grade writing); but Tionna's texts often included features of AAL. And yet
her home language was a major resource for her writing; AAL was the language
of her stories, her dreams, even her verbal play with other children. Moreover,
Tionna's sociolinguistic flexibility in both oral and written language should allow
her continuing expansion of her communicative repertoire (for a discussion of
curricular supports for such expansion, see Chapter 2).

The 1st-grade "standards" also included sentence-level punctuation marks,
among them periods, question marks, and exclamation points. For example, children were to "use periods at the ends of statements and in abbreviations such as
Mrs., Ms., and Dr." (Moats, 2004, p. 279). Tionna did not meet these standards

either, despite much explicit instruction and feedback. In this, she was similar to many young children (e.g., Cazden, Cordeiro, & Giacobbe, 1992). Still, some children, like Ezekial, were conventional users of sentence-level punctuation. As attuned as Tionna was to voices, Ezekial was attuned to visual symbols in and out of school, many of which were not listed on any 1st-grade punctuation list; these included those based in popular pleasures, like sports media, which were often found in his drawings (e.g., conventions of score reporting, football-field layouts, and uniform displays).

Ezekial also wrote short, simple sentences—typically three per text, the 1st-grade minimum-length requirement. Tionna wrote syntactically complex sentences that would have been difficult for more experienced writers to punctuate. Who is the more "advanced" writer, the child who meets "basic standards"? Is it possible to say? Perhaps they are following different routes, as Clay (1998) would say, to written language use.

THE RELEVANCE OF WRITING TO CHILDHOODS

At lunch, (Mrs. Lubbers) pulled me into the teachers' lounge, un-packed her lunch on the table, and made me identify each object.
. . . Then she pointed out the obvious packaging. Everything was tagged with its name, in clear, concise advertising. . . . She called the grocery story a public library. . . . "We are surrounded by words," she said. . . . "It's impossible not to read in this day and age. Not with all the Bazooka Joe comics lying around!"

—Sufjan Stevens (2007, p. xiv–xv)

In Sufjan Stevens's story, an adult is recalling a childhood of laissez-faire early schooling, followed by mind-numbing flash-card drills. Mrs. Lubbers finally got him on the path to written language by telling him to pay attention to the world and how it worked, beginning with "the literature of the advertising world" (p. xv), with its "antibacterial action," its "pain relief," and its "CAUTIONS," among other startling feats.

The children in this chapter were not in laissez-faire settings (quite the opposite), but their engagement with written language was also linked to the texts, written and otherwise, woven into their daily lives. We have stressed children's agency, the ways in which they pay attention to, find resources for, and make relevant the tool of written language. In the vignettes shared herein, Tommy found a library of sorts on his city street, where his apartment declared its numbers, and traffic signs ordered people around. He transformed his street from the 2-dimensional space of a drawing into the 3-dimensional world of blocks. Along the way, his added signs suggested that his interaction with his teacher had alerted him to pay attention to, and to orchestrate his understandings of, street, print, and the English language.

Alicia's drawing and talk suggested that she found a library in important people's names, especially that of her dear friend Willo. She learned to write messages to Willo and to play on paper with her, even as she learned about the encoding system through interactions with her teacher. Some of Alicia's peers reduced the writing task by repeating similar sentences from one day to the next, and some sat and waited for adult help. But Alicia, sitting by Willo, had social work to do.

Finally, Tionna seemed alert to the expansive library of voices she heard, both familiar and new—the voices of her aunty and her grandma, her cousins and her friends, and of Mrs. Kay herself. In textual work beyond that referenced herein, she also voiced the language of books about appealing historical figures (e.g., Ruby Bridges), as well as her preacher's and grandmother's talk about God; she wrote as a vulnerable princess needing saving, inspired by a Pokémon video and, of course, as a tough girl warrior in a cartoonlike space war. This alertness to voices was a major resource for her writing.

Each child was different, and not only in grade level. Collectively, however, they underscore significant themes in our consideration of young children, written language, and diversity. One such theme is that, for the children we have known, everyday relationships are interwoven with texts, including texts from the popular media (Marsh, 2003). These everyday texts are situated within both family practices—such as daily travel down familiar streets, grocery shopping, and sports media watching—and peer practices—like the communal Pine Cone Wars, with their roots in traditional chase games and space-age cartoons. And they are often multimodal and potentially multilingual (e.g., videos with captions in a home language, or first language newspapers with photos of popular figures [Kenner, 2005]).

Having family rituals involving school-condoned literature is clearly a worthy practice, but it is not the only one that allows our children to have experiences interpreting, identifying with, acquiring information from, and playing with texts (Robinson & Mackey, 2003). Indeed, from everyday multimodal experiences, children appropriate varied "textual toys" (Dyson, 2003, p. 10)—appealing content (e.g., movie characters and plot lines), intriguing communicative forms with varied graphic conventions (e.g., score boards and sports reports, weather maps and warnings, friendly letters and celebratory cards), and even characters' voiced utterances, all of which can be used to construct texts for varied ends.

For educators, then, attention to the stuff of children's lives is a key to engaging the "unengaged," so to speak, in the play (and work) of composing (Kamler & Comber, 2005; Marsh, 1999; Marsh & Millard, 2000). For this reason, we have stressed that children not only need teacher guidance in learning to write, but they also need time, materials, and one another to find ways to make writing relevant to their lives. And while it is important that teachers model and guide children's engagement with diverse genres across the curriculum (see Alice, a science aficionado, in Chapters 2 and 3 and in Stires & Genishi, 2008), it is also important to provide child-controlled time and space in which they may reveal semiotic resources, supportive relationships, and unanticipated communicative practices.

The above comment leads to another key theme: In the interplay of official and unofficial worlds, children may use written language in "relevant" ways that seem nonsensical or even unsuitable in the official world. Tommy's language play could seem just a waste of time, mere silliness; Alicia's sister play would not be on anyone's list of required activities, nor should it be; and Tionna's war play was unsettling to Mrs. Kay, and for good reason.

Young children tend to be drawn to other children and to play. So, as they sit side by side, their relationships and practices get all wound up with their use of the communicative tools at hand. For many children, this is a major avenue toward making writing relevant. Because children appropriate cultural material from adult-dominated worlds, it should be no surprise that they, like us, grapple with human relationships, like friendship, love, and battles (metaphoric or otherwise), and with societal structures, like gender and race. Their ideological assumptions (e.g., the proper roles of boys and girls) can be found in their characters and story lines and in their notions of who has the right to play on certain textual playgrounds.

Indeed, because children, like adults, are differently positioned in the social world, they have different vantage points on these issues, as did, for example, Tionna and Lyron. Moreover, Tionnna and Lyron's good friend Janette, like Mrs. Kay, associated "fake" war (to use Lyron's term) with "real" war and did not want to play. Given an official outlet, such unofficial tensions can be powerful pedagogical moments.

After all, playing a chase game on the playground is not the same as enacting that game through writing for the classroom public. Teachers and peers both might wonder about the sense, not to mention the worthiness, of the plot and the motivation as well as the gender of characters (and of authors). Such questions are not usually considered part of the official "basics." And yet they might bring children to the heart of what it means to be a socio-ideologically aware writer (Bakhtin, 1981): understanding that, through writing, one is not only interacting with, or amusing, others, but also positioning oneself in a world in which all do not agree.

We have also stressed that children's efforts to make sense of and use written language are neither uniform nor static. Children's writing varies because they have different linguistic and cultural resources, different situational goals, and varied social involvements; moreover, they face different curricular demands and, thus, have different ways of managing the complex dimensions of written language. Alicia in particular illustrated how children's ways of orchestrating their knowledge and know-how may vary. Sitting by Willo, she focused on playing with and pleasing her good friend and, also, accommodating her desires for a properly written (and read) name. Sitting with Mrs. Bee, she faced increasing demands for "big girl" writing, as Mrs. Bee had said. Alicia formed a manageable utterance and leaned on her teacher for help retrieving and orchestrating her written language knowledge. Without Mrs. Bee, she would need her peers to join in and help her write—although the goal could seem more one-upmanship or communal puzzle-solving than helpfulness. (For a related vignette of a Spanish writer, see Samway's [2006] account of Diana, based on Serna & Hudelson, 1993.)

Tionna, our most experienced writer, illustrated sociolinguistic flexibility. In ways akin to Tommy, she demonstrated that writing could be a way of playing with and examining language, as well as a mediator of communal play. Potentially such play could be pedagogically exploited by marrying attention to graphic symbols—Ezekial's forte—with attention to voices. Mrs. Kay's children generally seemed experienced enough writers to learn that ways of spelling and ways of speaking are not necessarily the same and that, in storybooks, literary artists sometimes use this symbolic feature (i.e., deliberately manipulate spelling conventions) to capture ways of speaking, as did Lucille Clifton (1992) in that storybook Tionna judged full of grammatical errors, *Three Wishes* (see Chapter 2). In fact, many of Mrs. Kay's children, whether or not they consistently used syntax-based conventions like periods, did manipulate spelling to capture qualities of the human voice, especially in dialogue bubbles; for example, drawn figures elongated their sounds (e.g., "Boooooo. . . .") and "yelled" in CAPITAL letters.

Children's varied resources and vantage points can thus potentially enrich one another's learning. Nonetheless, this variability means that children may respond more readily to one kind of event rather than another; moreover, events themselves support differing kinds of interaction and exploration. This leads us, finally, to this implied theme: teachers must be decision-makers, ultimately collaborating with children to enact a living curriculum; and this is so because any individual child may benefit from different kinds of curricular activities, with different kinds of interactional partners, and different possibilities of symbolic media.

This last theme is a striking disconnect from much current school policy, with its paced, mandated curriculum. Mrs. Bee, Alicia's teacher, felt that disconnect strongly; she was new to the district, anxious to make sure that her children met the expected benchmarks. At the same time, she worried that children lacked opportunities to play, to draw, and to use constructive materials; these were major language-generating activities and, moreover, ones that allowed children to make decisions and reveal their "personalities." (She no doubt would have felt curricularly at home in Ms. Yung's room.) Mrs. Bee was concerned, too, that certain trusted literacy activities were not stressed in her curriculum. Her worries recall those of Marie Clay, who argued that whenever we limit curricular options, we are in danger of limiting some children's possibilities for learning.

Mrs. Bee's district mandates stressed that children should write by sounding out words and inventing spellings, a potentially powerful tool but a complex one for various reasons (including reasons related to variation in pronunciation among the vernaculars of English and among children becoming bilingual). As Clay noted, Charles Read (1975) analyzed preschoolers' "invented" spellings based on phonological knowledge, but he did not show that this was how all young children begin to write, nor, we add, did he show that phonological knowledge was all that was needed for young children to find relevant and meaningful the complex tool of written language.

Mrs. Bee sometimes felt that she should take dictation or at least partial dictation of a child's story; a focus on message might be especially useful for storytellers like Alicia who have much to say; for children needing opportunities for extended conversation; and for those grappling with the process of writing, including fundamental concepts like how a message is composed of words and how each voiced word is matched to a bit of print. But dictation was not in her district guidelines.

Mrs. Bee also knew that individual children might take a special interest in particular words, and these words were another means for taking some control of writing. For example, Alicia had "key words," to use Ashton-Warner's (1963) term; these important words were names, most especially "Willo." (Mrs. Bee was searching for materials to instigate a classroom mailbox, which might provide a reason for writing names.) In Ms. Yung's room, Tommy had words that were not only known but literally tied to his home and his city street. Such words—or even letters, like Tatie's *T*—can be held onto when a child is adrift in a sea of print. These symbols are contributors to children's knowledge, resources to draw upon and weave with other knowledge and know-how gained from other activities involving print throughout the schoolday.

Like Mrs. Bee, Mrs. Kay worried, too. She wondered if she "modeled [writing] too much," even though modeling personal narratives was a routinized part of the curriculum; she worried that it limited children's opportunity to explore and use ways of writing that were meaningful to them. She also thought a lot about the "1st-grade paper"—its assumptions about the placement and relationship of picture and text and how that channeled the options that children had. And Anne, witnessing the Pine Cone Wars, could not help but think of another classroom, that of primary grade teacher Kristin Stringfield. The boys in her class wrote superhero stories full of fighting, and those stories were acted out in an Author's Theater, similar to how dictated stories were enacted in Mrs. Paley's room. The enacted superhero stories were thus opened up to public discussions of the gendered and racialized nature of certain characters, the sensibleness of the plot, the place of "action" (that is, fighting) in a story, and conceptions of power, including links to powerful nonviolent historical figures—just a sampling of the issues that arose (Dyson, 1997). But, in Mrs. Kay's packed and paced curriculum, there was no space for drama.

There is a false assumption that uniformity of instruction yields equality of outcome; but equality of instruction means that all children have the opportunity to develop in the only way possible—by building on what they know. Children's ability to do this depends not only on their own experiences and predilections but also on "what people in the environment are stressing" (Clay, 1998, p. 89). Providing a diversity of activities, joining in and helping children accomplish their intentions, and also providing time and space for children to collaborate, converse, and otherwise control the medium—in these ways we are more apt to learn what our children know and can do, and they are more apt to mobilize their resources and take intentional action through this flexible, powerful tool.

Thus, we are troubled by the notion that the surest way to close "gaps" between low-income children, disproportionately children of Color, and more affluent children is to explicitly (from the teacher's point of view) teach and formally test very young children on the conventional basics (e.g., letter names and sounds, handwriting, "proper" grammar). Although children need teachers' help, including their modeling, guiding, and provision of information, isolated "basics" do not add up to the dynamic, intention-driven act of composing. Moreover, as any teacher knows, what is explicitly taught is refracted as individual children make sense of what is offered. They "receive . . . the part that is meaningful to each individual . . . for further construction," and that includes what they choose to attend to (Clay, 1998; Nelson, 2007, p. 265). Rather than uniform, scripted teaching, children need observant teachers who can attune their teaching—their guiding interaction—to what children are doing.

We worry as well that curricular constraints and testing pressures will be visited on interaction itself, on children's and teachers' time to talk about words and worlds (about, say, butterflies' life cycle and the consequences of "segregation"), time for children to stretch their language and enact new roles and new ways of talking in play, and time for telling stories of some length, perhaps with performative zeal and imaginative vision—all communicative practices that can couch children's entry into literacy.

Our society, through its early childhood programs, may thus reduce language, literacy, and children themselves to checklists of basic skills and in the process lose sight of the most "basic" writing skill of all—the capacity for social participation and effective communication. In writing, as in speaking, this means the capacity to read a social situation and to adapt one's symbolic and cultural resources so as to have one's say. Over time, we aim for children who can differentiate, and make decisions about using, those complex and dynamic dimensions of the written system. For example, we want children to be able to make decisions about graphic features, like print SIZE, style, and arrangement, to consider the possibilities and constraints *de usar lenguajes distintos* and different modes, or to ponder the use of different genres or "voices" (Bakhtin, 1986). And, as always with young children, one reaches such a goal by beginning where the children are, with their own experiences as communicators and symbolizers. So we end this chapter as we began it, with the sentiments of Cohen's fictional 1st-grade teacher and an urge to focus on what our children can do.

6. Assessing Children's Language and Literacy

Dilemmas in Time

—

> You must work quickly.
> But do not worry—
> You can do it.
> Ready! Begin!
>
> —Miriam Cohen (1980/2006, n.p.)

With these words of exhortation, Cohen's fictional 1st-grade teacher sets her children on the path of their first standardized test—an academic race to a timed finish. Surely the teacher's feelings are conflicted and match her words—on the one hand, confident that the children "can do it," and on the other, worried, herself, that they won't have enough time. In this idyllic classroom the teacher counters the adverse effects—squabbles among the children, for one—of test taking, through humane, common-sense actions. She provides a curriculum that enables children to demonstrate their abilities; these are what she wants to assess, whether or not they are addressed on the test.

We authors admit that we also feel pressured by the 1st-grade teacher's exhortation, given that the topic of tests and, more generally, assessment is so broad—we are hoping to have enough time and space in one chapter to address relevant issues that we know are a source of worry to many.

On to what assessment means in the classroom. The word *assessment* provokes teachers' varied reactions, from resistance and avoidance ("Oh no, we don't assess our children") to matter-of-fact acceptance ("They can't tell if children are learning if we don't assess them"). Both the avoider and the accepter have a narrow definition of the term *assessment*—that is, standardized tests that "they" have mandated. In this chapter we use the term broadly to include, at one end of the assessment framework, the ways by which teachers and other adults observe and document children's learning and, at the other end, standardized tests.

We frame the chapter by first elaborating on the current time, on the pressures teachers now feel to focus on standardized tests and the narrowly defined curriculum that tests measure. We then turn to early childhood teachers who in their own words tell about assessing unique children in nonstandardized ways in particular classroom contexts. We collectively address varying dilemmas regarding time and space, as teachers in preschool and kindergarten enact—live through—definitions of assessment and "intervention." As stressed in Chapter 5, and indeed throughout our book, we envision teachers as decision-makers, not technicians or test administrators. Their decisions are grounded in the observations—and assessments—they make as part of the daily work of teaching.

ASSESSMENT IN THESE POSTMODERN TIMES

We begin, then, with a conceptual framework that is spacious enough for starkly different meanings of the term *assessment*. Recall that in Chapter 3 we discussed two kinds of time: NCLB or panoptical time (Lesko, 2001), compressed time that is oriented toward narrowly defined ends like test scores, and in contrast, unhurried time, which we hope children experience as learners, according to their inner clocks.

We also mentioned the multitemporal teacher as time switcher, one who knows when to speed up and when to slow down, an ability that the fictional 1st-grade teacher appears to have. This multitemporal teacher can interpret which kind of time is appropriate for children in classrooms where she arranges for unhurried child-oriented activities, yet is required to give rigidly timed tests.

Flexible curriculum squeezed in around firm things like mandated tests and standards may be considered the *postmodern* face of educational phenomena— that is, the phenomena are eclectic, indeterminate, without fixed standards, and full of multiple, sometimes contradictory, perspectives to which people of diverse and shifting social identities, like the children and teachers we have introduced you to, are expected to adjust (Sarup, 1993).

Here we attempt to think multitemporally ourselves, to focus on NCLB or panoptical time and then on unhurried—or at least less hurried—time and the assessments associated with it. We turn first to NCLB time and its consequences, such as the standardized tests that few children are able to avoid. These tests grew out of the field of *measurement,* which aims to assess or evaluate by assignment of a number, using clearly identified and objective procedures (Thorndike & Hagen, 1977). Related terms are often defined in the following ways:

assessment—a term reserved for determinations about people, usually individuals (sometimes small groups);
evaluation—operations associated with nonperson entities, such as curricula, programs, interventions, methods of teaching, and organizational factors. (Keeves, 1994, p. 363)

The traditional way to assess groups of students is to administer a standardized
test. We turn next to some ways in which standardized testing is negatively affect-
ing the youngest students, despite the best efforts of multitemporal teachers.

The Impact of Federal Policies: Something Is Terribly Wrong

In recent decades teachers at all age and grade levels have been challenged
to hold in mind standards imposed by the school or district and state or federal
government, along with their own standards, which they hope will fit the group
of unique individuals in their classrooms or centers. The No Child Left Behind
(NCLB) Act of 2001 refers to federal legislation in the United States that provides
funds for and mandates specific policies for elementary and secondary education
(see Elementary and Secondary Education Act of 1965 for background). NCLB
had an immediate and blunt impact because of its mandates for standardized
testing. Its funding arm, Reading First, has also reshaped the way that reading is
taught, because only phonics-oriented programs have been funded. (See Chrismer, Hodge, & Saintil, 2006; Garan, 2004; Goodman, 2006; Meier & Wood,
2004; Nichols & Berliner, 2007, for a range of commentary and critique on the
impact of NCLB.)

Cochran-Smith and Lytle (2006) concisely summarize the blatant effects of
NCLB on how teachers teach, children learn, and teachers are educated:

> NCLB is changing how we, the educational community, the policy com-
> munity, and the public, think about teachers and teaching. Like it or not,
> supporting or resisting, believing or doubting, diverse stakeholders in the
> educational process are coming to regard teachers as technicians, student
> learning as performance on tests, and teacher learning as frontal training
> and re-training on what works. NCLB is pervasive and strategic in its logic,
> using simple, direct language and relentless repetition to present and re-
> present an impermeable logic about how to fix the schools by fixing teachers
> and teaching. (p. 689)

This is not good news; and unfortunately it is not new news, as many of us saw
these changes for the worse well before the passage of NCLB in early childhood
classrooms. Here we will not dwell on the overbearing reach of NCLB since, as
we said earlier, the components of its reauthorization are in doubt as this book

goes to press. By placing it in a broad context, we hope to illuminate the impact of such policies on language and literacy learning and teaching.

How the News Is Worse: Reducing Children to "Readers"

When children's learning is measured by one kind of assessment—performance on standardized tests—we know that there will be consequences. For example, the classroom curriculum will change—that is, what teachers plan to teach and the ways in which their plans actually unfold in the classroom change. In turn, the learner is changed: Instead of children who are simultaneously players, learners, readers of the world and words, artists—among other identities—children are now increasingly viewed in care and education settings solely as prospective *students*. This narrow identity is not just a consequence of the NCLB legislation. Indeed, toddlers have been potential students for decades, taking school entrance tests in places like New York City (see Stracher, 1999, where he laments the lack of acceptance of his two-and-a-half-year-old into desirable nursery schools, following an exhausting application process).

Moreover, when policy makers declared that Head Start should become an early reading program (Bumiller, 2003), they began to speak into existence children with an even more diminished identity than that of student; the children became further reduced to narrowly defined "readers." This reductionist view of children grows out of a reductionist view of written language and what it means to become readers and writers.

As we noted in Chapter 5, written language is a complex, multidimensional tool that children come to use as social beings with individual histories and interests. Thus, although we wholeheartedly agree that all children should learn to read and write, we object to reducing literacy learning to a list of skills to be tested. Instead, we place in the foreground the broad goal of communicative flexibility, of which mastering skills is but a small part.

We can trace the shrinking of child identity to "reader" in kindergarten through Grade 2 as we look at the influence of a single standardized test, DIBELS, or Dynamic Indicators of Basic Early Literacy Skills (Good & Kaminski, 2002). It defines reading narrowly in the same way that Reading First administrators and the creators of reading programs funded by Reading First do. Accordingly, reading has five components, or as the authors of DIBELS call them, Big Ideas—phonological awareness, alphabetic principle, fluency with text, comprehension, and vocabulary. These are indeed very big ideas, though defined in small ways within constraints (Goodman, 2006), such as the narrow limits of panoptical time. For example, children must identify letters and read words quickly, and teachers are instructed to time children with a stopwatch while administering these DIBELS subtests. There could be no better example of NCLB time!

Looking to ever younger children, the creators of Early Reading First (2002) fashioned a federal literacy program for preschool children. The program was developed in league with Reading First and Good Start, Grow Smart (2002) so that teachers can teach young children the skills incorporated in DIBELS even before they enter elementary school. According to federal guidelines, centers or schools funded by Early Reading First should identify pre-kindergartners who are at risk of failing at reading and then help the children to attain early reading skills using scientifically based curricula (Early Reading First, 2002). They will also be taught the skills to be successful students in kindergarten.

In the field of early childhood education, the professional stance has been that standardized tests should only be given for children to qualify for special services, so a test of early reading skills might meet this qualification (Bredekamp & Shepard, 1989; Gullo, 2005; National Center for Infants, Toddlers, & Families, 1997). The overly focused curriculum of Early Reading First, though, begs the question of whether these are "services" that should be provided for or, more accurately, imposed on children. It begs the question, too, of why a comprehensive program for children and families like Head Start should become so narrowly defined, marked by assessment of early reading skills.

Standardized assessments spelled out in federal guidelines easily get proclaimed and written into existence. Indeed, a computer-based test is already in use to identify young children who are at "high risk" for reading problems. There is even a handheld computer called "M-Class: Circle" to see if children can do rhyming exercises or tell whether pairs of words sound the same or different (O'Neil, 2006).

The mildest thing we can say about this process of early identification is that it's a puzzler, because when children are 3 or 4 years of age, they typically are not conventional readers, especially not with the ability to manipulate sounds or separate sounds of words from their meanings. And if they are EBs like Alice, Luisa, or Miguel, they are just entering the social world of the classroom through talk in a language other than English. How would any of them have performed on M-Class: Circle in English as 3- or 4-year-olds? Should the ability to rhyme and recognize similar or different sounds really precede the acquisition of spoken language for pre-kindergartners, regardless of home language? To drop the mildness, we think that this process of testing for supposed deficits in pre-kindergartners is ridiculous!

Instead of assuming that pre-K teachers' responsibility is to introduce skills within an active, child-oriented curriculum, teachers are required to label some children as low or "potentially struggling readers" from the start. That is the core of norm-based, standardized tests: By definition, some children must fall below the norm. They must demonstrate what they are *not* able to do so that their school districts will receive funding. The funding in turn enables teachers to teach them the needed skills, and at the end of the year the children will take another test to demonstrate how much they've learned. In kindergarten and in later years some children take the test three times a year and also may have monthly tests tethered to the teaching of skills. Along the way, test publishers and those who write the tests earn considerable amounts of money (Allington, 2002). And so the testing cycles go—this process is called *accountability.*

The further consequences of this obsession for testing could be described as follows:

- Where there used to be early childhood curricula with read-alouds of children's literature, there may be structured phonics lessons.
- Where there used to be chunks of time for play and child-chosen activities, there may be 90-minute literacy blocks.
- Where there were children free to "explore with a pencil" (Clay, 1977) and to draw, play, and talk their way into written language, there may be paced writing programs that reduce composing to spelling.
- Where there were teachers who created their own assessments of children's progress, there may be standardized tests three times a year or more.

Through this less-than-subtle process, some adults, caught up in panoptical time, feel compelled to make children into narrowly defined "readers."

Teachers Assessing Children: Diverse Time Lines on Classroom Stages

> Science cannot utter a single word about the individual molecule, thing, or creature (or child) insofar as it is an individual but only insofar as it is like other individuals.
>
> —Walker Percy (cited in Cole, 1986, p. vii)

With NCLB and its consequences as a backdrop, you may question whether our conceptual framework is really postmodern, whether practices and policies are eclectic, and whether unhurried time exists alongside the panoptical time surrounding so many tests. We acknowledge the dominance of standardized tests, benchmarks for moving children from one grade to the next or, to paraphrase Walker Percy, Science's way of stating how one child is like or unlike a group of other children. Yet these tests have not been accepted without question. Along with standards, relationships of power have become fluid, and those who have the power to assert standards and theories underlying them face multiple challenges. For decades the legitimacy of standardized tests has been questioned (see, e.g., Baratz & Baratz, 1970; Gould, 1996; Kohn, 2000), even by protesting students (Hartocollis, 2002). Thus the powerful "grand narrative" (Lyotard, 1984) of objective assessment now competes with many narratives or teacher-based judgments in tune with these eclectic and diverse times.

"Objective" test administrators take an impartial and scientific stance, and they purposely know nothing about individual children in the classroom. This means that teachers' assessments are conceptually opposed to traditional testing in a range of ways, mainly because teachers work hard to know individual learners, guided by the planned, spontaneous, and often idiosyncratic events of their classrooms. In short, teachers-as-assessors are not on the outside looking in. Rather, as insiders, they are continually with the children being assessed and metaphorically within the learners' minds.

The image of the teacher with children calls up the Latin root of the verb to *assess*—that is, *assidere,* to sit beside (Casper & Theilheimer, in press), an intimate image worthy of Cohen's now-familiar 1st-grade teacher and her children. We think she would agree with our definition of *assessment:*

> An ongoing, complex process in which we aim to discover and document what children are learning over time in many situations and across multiple symbol systems, so that we can help them learn more.

As you saw, the children in earlier chapters illustrate diverse meanings of "learning over time." Thus, in response to the overall question "How is this particular group of EBs learning languages in school settings?", we conclude that children take varying amounts of time to become social and linguistic beings. For example, Tommy in Chapter 3 is an enthusiastically social and rapid learner of English. The segment of his assessment time line representing his entry into the world of spoken English, then, lasts a few months, whereas Alice, Luisa, and Miguel develop spoken languages slowly over more than a year of unhurried time.

As we also emphasized earlier, in the same educational spaces where children are learning one or more languages over time, we ask, "How do children show their knowledge and know-how across countless situations, in their many kinds of play, as they use different language forms and language(s)?" In short, how do they demonstrate their sociolinguistic flexibility? You saw that children who are not EBs also follow different assessment time lines. For example, Tionna in Chapter 5, always a speaker of AAL and now in 1st grade, has already stepped off the out-of-classroom stage of very early childhood on to a classroom stage with different curricular demands. There she demonstrates what she is able to do with varied language forms and styles, across official and unofficial curricular situations. As always we reach the assessment goal of seeing what children like Tionna or Luisa are able to do by beginning *where the children are.* As we see next, it is observation that helps us find that space.

Ways of Assessing: Observing as the Foundation

We look back to Chapters 3 and 5 to offer a brief sketch of how teacher-based assessment might look. Recall the series of notes that Ariela and Celia took while observing Miguel and Luisa in their Head Start rooms (see Figure 3.1). And recall that the children appeared to experience unhurried time, allowing us to "see," in Georgia O'Keeffe's sense, small and large behaviors and changes. Our method was primarily observation, defined broadly: "To observe is to take notice, to pay attention to what children do and say" (Almy & Genishi, 1979, p. 21).

For teachers this kind of observation is ongoing and becomes a habit of the mind and senses that ingrains itself over time. Observant teachers see or hear behaviors, and in addition often sense the "vibes" of each day, perhaps of each minute. They observe to see what children are able to do—and because teachers aim to help children learn, they also ask what the children are *not* able to do in particular tasks and events, with their shifting purposes, participants, and symbolic tools.

For example, Mrs. Bee, whom we discussed in Chapter 5, was under pressure to get her kindergartners such as Alicia to invent spellings, thereby demonstrating their sound-symbol knowledge. She observed how Alicia wrote and, in response, gradually made new demands on her. But Mrs. Bee knew that Alicia's alphabetic knowledge was not a clear-cut matter. Her encoding processes and her messages shifted along with events' participants and purposes. A string of letters and a dear friend's name, along with a picture, could convey that pretend sister's place in her life, even in her dreams. But messages were simplified even as encoding processes were made more complex when she wrote with, and for, her teacher. If Mrs. Bee had judged Alicia only by what she wrote "on her own," she could easily have underestimated Alicia's knowledge (i.e., her "zone of proximal development" [Vygotsky, 1978, p. 84]); and if Mrs. Bee had not observed Alicia's friendship with Willo, she might have dismissed—or completely missed—the significance of the latter child's perfectly spelled name as it snuggled in among Alicia's letters.

So ongoing observation is part of an active and complex cycle of observing or assessing and planning the next curricular steps in a highly situated way. Unlike researchers, who are often not interactive, teachers are observers who weave observation into interactions. Therefore, this is not observation as surveillance, to see whether children are violating rules (though children's safety is a concern) or whether their performance matches a checklist from a mandated curriculum or a developmental stage theory (Campbell & Smith, 2001). Rather, it is observation that leads to learning more about children's knowledge and know-how in particular situations and to helping them learn more. And the learning that happens over time is part of each child's assessment time line. (For more on the complex connections among observation, learning, and teaching, see Cohen, Stern, Balaban, & Gropper, 2008; Genishi, 1992; Genishi & Dyson, 1984; Jablon, Dombro, & Dichtelmiller, 2007; Meisels, 2002; Shepard, 2006).

Looking to teachers' know-how—how they manage to observe in the midst of the layers of unofficial and official classroom activity—we consider some ways that teachers document what they notice:

- Scraps of paper or index cards where teachers describe what a child like Miguel constructed with blocks. These scraps or cards are often stuffed inside a pocket, file folder, or envelope, where they await the teacher's reading or organizing.
- Stenographers' notepads or small pads of paper that have a line down the middle, either printed on the page or drawn by the teacher. On one side are observations or field notes, perhaps describing the behaviors of a child like Luisa; and on the other, comments or questions that are written when there is a moment to reflect on the meanings of her nonverbal behaviors.
- Stickies or Post-its, to which no one needs an introduction. These may later be assembled in a notebook or on sheets of paper or written up in greater detail in a journal or computer file. They may even be placed on a child's paper, perhaps one saved in a portfolio. Stickies can remind a teacher of contextual details, like whom a child like Alicia talked with as she wrote.
- Cameras and electronic aides, like audio or video recorders, which have the virtue of permanence but have the disadvantage of taking time to process or transcribe. PDAs (personal digital assistants) or handheld computers enable an immediate transcription, but may be distracting. (For details related to visual documentation of children's learning in the tradition of Reggio Emilia, see Cadwell & Rinaldi, 2003; Helm, Beneke, & Steinheimer, 2007; Wurm, 2005.)

Of course, the content of the notes or documents is what matters, along with teachers' purposes for observing, or the questions they are asking about their children. In the next sections pre-kindergarten and kindergarten teachers illustrate such purposes. They capture long and short segments of assessment time lines that focus on particular children on varied classroom stages. We aim to make the abstraction of an assessment time line concrete as teachers sit beside, stand with, and interact with their child learners and those children's families while they assess the sociolinguistic flexibility of children who are both like and unlike Tionna, Miguel, Luisa, and Alice. Once again we stress that teachers' views of children's learning are always mediated by contextual conditions; children do not speak, read, or write on an abstract time line but, rather, they respond as active agents to their own interpretations of the fluid goings-on of classroom life.

TEACHERS' ASSESSMENT IN PRESCHOOL: COLLABORATORS HAVING THEIR SAY

A number of years ago Celia collaborated with a group of preschool teachers who began their first conversation about assessment by saying, "We don't assess our children." After many more conversations, the teachers revised their judgment and decided that they assessed all the time, though in informal ways. The collaboration between the teachers and Celia has continued, as have the teachers' informal ways of assessing. At the School for Young Children (SYC), a private preschool in Columbus, Ohio, the staff has the luxury of choosing a curriculum that they believe supports children's development and learning in unhurried ways (Waters, Frantz, Rottmayer, Trickett, & Genishi, 1992). Classroom activities are play-based, like the curriculum at Luisa and Miguel's Head Start.

Indeed, the principles undergirding SYC and the Head Start center are strikingly similar: children's social, emotional, and language development is as important as their cognitive and academic learning; and play, as we noted in Chapter 4, allows children to have a say in the curriculum and to learn skills that are sociolinguistic and cognitive. In other words, these two early childhood settings demonstrate that there are sites of resistance to the dominance of outsider testing and its companion, narrowly defined early reading curricula.

Since their first collaboration with Celia, the SYC teachers have had further thoughts about formal assessment and how it focuses on what a child is lacking, not on a child's strengths. They would agree with Cohen's fictional 1st-grade teacher that children have many abilities that vary from child to child, despite the prevalence of one-size-fits-all testing. Getting to know a child is a part of assessing that the SYC teachers have always fit into their curriculum planning, often in the form of stories. Jan Waters, teacher and former SYC director, tells the following story in the fall of 2007.

Dominic (Jan's Story)

The first day of school this year, Dominic is playing hockey in a danger-ous way. He has fascinating energy but it looks as if someone will die. I want to get to know this kid. So I put my clipboard down and draw a hockey court on the sidewalk. Dominic can hardly stop playing to listen to me, but I become a coach and call the hockey team over. I ask the name of the teams—Superheroes and Power Rangers—and I draw an X in the middle of the court. I make a scoreboard for the teams. "Here is where to start," I say. Three boys including Dominic play vigorous hockey with only a few reminders to stay in the court. No one gets killed or even hurt. I assess Dominic to have great physical skills and a big desire to play with others. He shows interest in literacy by naming his team, and he has some difficulty listening to an adult (not unusual for a 4-year-old boy with a lot of energy). I learned a lot about this very interesting boy and I like him.

So we believe that our most useful source of assessment is careful daily observation. We find out what a kid's interests and strengths are and build on that. What we are looking at is the child's own individual milestones. We are watching to see how each child develops as an individual.

Thus Jan observes to see where children are and informally documents their assessment time lines. Teachers at SYC seek individuals' milestones in, for example, physical or language development and aim to see abilities along with weaknesses, interests along with indifference. As we discussed in Chapter 5, young children's daily lives are often infused with graphic symbols, and those symbols are potential resources for children and teachers. Given a quiet mo-ment to reflect on Jan's short story about Dominic, we see how sophisticated the three boys are, and we also note the potential resources grounded in their popular interests: The children easily appropriated names from popular culture (Superheroes and Power Rangers), while they responded to the graphic symbols of sports—for example, the "X" that marked the spot to start their game and the lines that bounded their court. With this story Jan shows how observa-tion can quickly lead to action and interaction, not an attitude of surveillance. Stories like these also illustrate how integral frequent observation is to the SYC insiders' ways of assessing. (For an appreciation of stories and "voices inside schools," especially Vivian Paley's [2007a, 2007b], see the special issue with that title of the *Harvard Educational Review,* 2007.)

As recounted below, Jan's colleague, Joanne Frantz, a head teacher of 3s and 4s, tells a different kind of story, which incorporates articulate voices within the school, as well as outside it. We—Anne and Celia—emphasize with humility that

Joanne and her colleagues are about to take us into a space that is not an area of expertise for either of us, that of early childhood special education. We have been learning alongside the SYC staff.

Allan, a Child with "Language Delay": Insiders and Outsiders Collaborate (Joanne and Gemma's Story)

Speaking about children in general, Jan provides a prelude to Joanne's story about Allan:

> There is such variation in development at the preschool age that "normal" ranges are unpredictable. But occasionally we observe a child that is so far out of the developmental ranges that we think he or she could use more specific help in certain areas. *Early intervention* has developed and improved greatly in the last 10 years (see Figure 6.1 for definitions related to special needs). We have seen that children with some developmental lags or disabilities benefit so much by being identified and given therapies as early as possible. So our attitude toward early intervention has become more trusting, and we have more interest in learning about *sensory integration* activities and visual cues that we can incorporate in our own teaching for all children.

FIGURE 6.1. Terms and Definitions Related to Autism and Very Young Children with Special Needs

---

Autism spectrum disorders (ASDs) "are a class of neurodevelopmental disorders characterized by an impairment in social reciprocity, atypical communication, and repetitive behaviors. The term autism spectrum indicates that the disorders in this category occur along a continuum and is commonly used as a synonym for the category *pervasive developmental disorders*" (PDD) (Hyman & Towbin, 2008, p. 325).

Diagnostic and Statistical Manual of Mental Disorders (DSM IV TR 2000). The standard reference for clinicians diagnosing "mental disorders," such as autism spectrum disorders (American Psychiatric Association, 2000).

Early intervention was originally a legal term, used in Part C of the Individuals with Disabilities Education Act (U.S. Department of Education, 2004). Such intervention is to support children between birth and age 3 with diagnosed special needs. The term is used more generally as well to refer to a range of interventions for children in this age range.

Sensory integration is a somewhat controversial set of interventions related to children's sensory processing or abilities to regulate themselves.

Allan's teacher Joanne tells his assessment story, which would not have happened without the collaboration of other knowledgeable adults, especially his mother Gemma, along with other teachers and the school's directors. Because of what appeared to be a language delay and lack of interaction with other children, Angela, his teacher in the 2s room, wondered whether he was showing signs of *autism*. Here is the beginning of the assessment story, in Joanne's words:

> Before school started last fall, Angela, one of our SYC 2s teachers, alerted me to her concerns about Allan, one of the children in our 3/4 class. Angela had noticed Allan had a severe language delay and lack of engagement with other children, which made her question whether he had problems with auditory processing or might be on the autism spectrum. Angela worked very hard to develop a relationship with Allan's parents by talking to them frequently about what she saw and inviting them to observe too. She had voiced her concern about his development and thought at year's end that he was scheduled to be tested by his suburban school district over the summer.
>
> Then, Allan attended our summer play camp before I taught him in the fall. His teachers reported that he often "escaped" or tried to escape from the 3s class to go outside when no teacher was there, and from the 3s playground onto other school playgrounds. They wondered if he understood or could process rules about space limits. They said Allan loved to paint at the easel and chase bubbles outside but seemed to be "in his own world" most of the time. They also reported he rarely spoke.
>
> As school began in September, our 3- and 4-year-old class included 18 children and 3 teachers. Before school I discussed with my co-teachers, Patti and Denise, the need for good communication with Allan's parents and documentation of his behavior. I was eager to establish a warm and positive relationship with Gemma, Allan's mother, who usually brought him to school. Stephanie, our director, already had a good relationship with the parents from the previous year because the dad had chaired our maintenance committee.

We note a number of important features of Allan's story thus far. First, the 2s teacher Angela and her colleagues together formulate the question of whether he might be on the autism spectrum. Second, the question leads to a number of teachers and an administrator communicating over time about what Allan is able to do with oral language, as well as what he's not able to do in the everyday setting of preschool. Third, Allan's parents have been a key part of the story, not only as a consequence of Allan's language delay, but because of a school committee that relied on parent volunteers. We move next to the gradual evolution of Allan's story.

Assessing Allan: Not a Straight-line Story

In keeping with postmodern acknowledgments of fluidity and indeterminacy in the everyday world, we note how much classroom assessments can vary for one child and across many children. Although a standardized test score is seen as fixed and permanent at a point in time, teachers' observations or documents are seen as moving pieces of a dynamic and complex story, like the notes taken over time about Allan's progress. Thus regular documentation of children's growing knowledge and know-how about language, whether oral or written, never leads to a straight-line story or assessment time line.

Allan's teachers routinely take quick notes on what he is and is not able to do; these are discussed at regular meetings with the director and other teachers at the school. Using oral language as his peers do is something he is not able to do. Thus Joanne's story includes Allan's interest in other children, especially when playing a chase game called "Duck, Duck, Goose," which requires Allan to run around a small circle but doesn't require him to converse. Allan's overall lack of language in the classroom, though, affects his ability to engage with peers, something that Joanne feels is critical for a three and a half year old. Allan can imitate classmates' silly noises or repeat single words that he hears, but he does not respond to questions or add to dialogue. Joanne then tells Gemma about these concerns. As the fall of 2006 ends, Allan is absent off and on.

Despite everyone's good intentions, the next phase of the story is most difficult because it is marked by miscommunication. Whereas Joanne is unsure whether Gemma has scheduled an appointment with a specialist, Gemma in fact started exploring the assessment process when Allan was still in the 2s room. After Joanne talks to Gemma about her concerns in the 3/4s class, Gemma talks immediately with his pediatrician and proceeds with the assessment process.

By December Gemma consults with a behavioral specialist at the local children's hospital who asks Joanne and Gemma to complete the Gilliam Autism Rating Scale (GARS-2, Gilliam, 2006). Based on those ratings, Allan is diagnosed with pervasive developmental disorder not otherwise specified (PDD-NOS), a diagnosis that is used when criteria for a specific disorder, such as Autistic Disorder are not met. Recall, for example, that Allan showed an interest in other children, a behavior not typical of children diagnosed with Autistic Disorder. The diagnosis of PDD-NOS becomes the key to Allan's parents learning about and selecting special classes for him outside of SYC. (For details on definitions and diagnostic criteria see Hyman & Towbin, 2007, and Zager, 2004. For examples of inclusive practices for young children on the autism spectrum, see Boulware, Schwartz, Sandall, & McBride, 2006, and for young children with significant disabilities, see Kliewer et al., 2004.)

After not communicating with Joanne in December, Gemma sends an e-mail to her on the first day of the new year, explaining what has happened, stating how very hard it is for her to write the message since she feels that "Allan is perfect." Joanne understands, but she also senses that Gemma is angry with her for not doing more for Allan in the classroom. Later Joanne learns that Gemma and her husband had decided that SYC was not a good fit for Allan and kept him at home in January. However, demonstrating his own sense of agency and ability to communicate, Allan himself insists on returning—and in February does so, after the school's director moderates a discussion between Allan's parents and Joanne. So on this nonlinear path toward helping Allan to become a communicator, communication between adults sometimes came to a halt. Ultimately, though, Allan returns to Joanne's classroom where Gemma acts as her son's advocate and coach, building on what she has observed in Allan's classes at a local speech and hearing center. Joanne and her co-teachers find Gemma's participation to be very helpful for Allan, his peers, and them as growing professionals.

The center that Allan attends specializes in "speech and social delays." He first participates there in a play group of four children with delays similar to his own, 3 times a week, and works with a speech therapist once a week. He later advances to a group of 11 children who work with an early childhood special education teacher, teacher's assistant, speech therapist, and occupational therapist. (The services of therapists and special educators are usually available to children in situations like Allan's.) Allan's parents have two conferences in the spring with Joanne when all share information about Allan's impressive progress and discuss the SYC teachers' plans for him. Gemma sums up this collaborative phase:

> This is the most interesting portion to me both as a parent with a non-ideal relationship with my son's teacher and with opportunities to see Allan's great gains and improvement. . . . I believe I learned from Joanne, and she hopefully learned from me.

The following year (2007–08), Allan's 4s year, he comes back to SYC for 2 days of the week and continues to receive speech and other therapy at the speech and hearing center.

This is a short version of a long and complex story, a story of teachers and parents—those closest to Allan—as decision makers, focused on a child whose assessment time line for communication and language is notably different from his peers'. Thus instead of descriptions of language-and-literacy-based interactions, like Jan's anecdote about Dominic, Joanne and Gemma offer the story behind a distinctive assessment time line shaped by insiders who invited outsider evaluation and intervention. In the end a bumpy and sometimes painful collaboration becomes smoother during a year of unhurried time. We began Allan's story with Joanne's words and close it with Gemma's. She and Allan's father are able to report a year later in the fall of 2008, with deep happiness and satisfaction, that Allan no longer needs special classes. As part of the older 4/5s room at SYC,

> Allan is a very talkative and imaginative 5-year-old kid with great social skills. He can say, "Hello, my name is Allan. Do you want to play Star Wars with me?" or "You're beautiful as the sun. Do you want to go to the movies with me?" He can engage in dialogue for more than 15 turns with no assistance and has many friends. Eye contact is no longer an issue. He will be attending typical kindergarten next year at age 6.

Assessing Allan: Some Benefits of Testing

Thinking back to the contrast between unhurried and NCLB time, it's clear that Allan's teachers were not pressured by the kinds of tests pre-kindergartners in publicly funded schools might take to demonstrate their early reading skills by the age of 4. Allan did not take a diagnostic test although his mother and teacher completed one (GARS-2), the kind approved by the National Association for the Education of Young Children (NAEYC/NAECS/SDE, 2003), by which testers determine in part what children are not able to do and whether they should receive particular services. The therapy that Allan was eligible for following the diagnosis of pervasive developmental disorder indeed helped him learn social and conversational skills, the benefit his parents and teachers longed to see—and, in time, did.

Allan's is a story with a happy ending. We know of other stories that do not follow the same path. School staff may make decisions without clear communication with parents or teachers, and children are labeled with stigmatizing cognitive or emotional disabilities. And the unhappy stories disproportionately involve children and families of color, more likely than not in schools on NCLB time. Our next assessment story takes us into such a school, where at least one teacher is able to influence the assessment time lines in her classroom so that children have a chance to shed labels and are assessed in ways close in spirit to those of the SYC teachers.

ASSESSMENT IN MS. HONG'S KINDERGARTEN CLASSROOM: A STORY-IN-AN-INTERVIEW

Jenny is a kindergartner in a New York City public school with about 500 children (kindergarten through Grade 5), the majority of whom are of Latino heritage. Like many of her peers, Jenny is an English Language Learner (the term used by the school and school district) so that she speaks Spanish on her first day of school. There is a schoolwide focus on literacy instruction, and the mandated program is the Reading/Writing Workshop approach (Calkins, 2003). According to Jenny's teacher, Min Hong, there is notable pressure to perform well on reading tests of all kinds. In short, theirs is a school on NCLB time.

Ms. Hong's educational focus for more than 15 years has been the young children in her classrooms (kindergarten through Grade 2). Like the other teachers we include, she is not "typical." She has remained in classrooms in New York City public schools far longer than most teachers (Boyd, Grossman, Lankford, Loeb, & Wyckoff, 2008), and she has published books for children and teachers (Hong, 2000, 2001). As a teacher-researcher, each year Ms. Hong chooses a "case-study child" who is in some way challenging. Her choice this year (2006–2007) is Jenny because in January the school's administrators label her as "struggling" and "at risk"—that is, in danger of being held over or retained in kindergarten at year's end.

Not long ago adults joked about children being retained in kindergarten: "What—did they flunk block building?" Unfortunately, many adults, including parents, are now accustomed to the idea that kindergarten is the year when children should begin to read, even if, according to their inner clocks, they are not ready (Graue, 2006). The view of Jenny as a potential "holdover" and "struggling reader" is quite different from Ms. Hong's view. She tends to see children with their proverbial glasses half-full. In Jenny she sees a smart and confident child who comes to her first school experience, kindergarten, speaking Spanish, her home language. Jenny also knows some numbers and is able to draw a picture of herself (see Figure 6.2).

In other words, Ms. Hong and Cohen's fictional 1st-grade teacher share the view that assessment begins with what children are able to do and where they are in the classroom space and in the stories they bring with them. Jenny's favorite story line early in the year centers on things she does with her mom. In Figure 6.3, for example, she is able to write the words *Mom* and *me,* and Ms. Hong writes the rest as Jenny dictates, "I am giving my mom flowers."

Keeping in mind that Jenny spoke little English in the first weeks of school, we see promising detail and cheerfulness in Jenny's artwork and writing, not symptoms of incipient struggle. In the next section we focus equally on what Jenny and Ms. Hong do, through a story-in-an-interview carried out in August of 2007, structured around questions from us and answers from Ms. Hong—and Jenny, through her work. We include the questions and responses that focus most clearly on Jenny and her literacy learning and Ms. Hong's assessment practices. Like many other teachers Ms. Hong is faced with the pressures of an increasingly academic curriculum where children are portrayed primarily as "readers"—or children who seem to be on the path toward becoming readers, those who are firmly on the path, and those who are "struggling" to find a foothold on that path.

FIGURE 6.2. Jenny's Self-Portrait and Numbers

FIGURE 6.3. Jenny Giving Her Mom Flowers

Next Ms. Hong talks about the different aspects of assessment: what *assessment* is and how she differentiates among children, works with them, and assesses them as part of her ongoing curriculum. Keep in mind that her knowledge and know-how come through years of experience with young children, their families, and colleagues. Remember, too, that teachers in similar situations might see and assess the same children in very different ways. We hope that our questions below are like your own. Our comments (Anne's and Celia's) are interspersed throughout in parentheses.

How Do You Define "Assessment"?

Basically for me *assessment* means not just observing and collecting what children are doing, but also taking it farther and taking it apart. I used to use the word *analyze,* but if I say "take it apart," that makes me look at things deeper. I was always confident, but now I think I'm less superficial. I use that information that I collect and put it right back into my teaching, into my curriculum. That's basically assessment for me—it's that simple.

(Simple, indeed! Ms. Hong said at another point in the interview, not presented here, that she's been working on assessing children well for at least 15 years, but the first 5 years shouldn't count, because she didn't know what she was doing. We know that she's exaggerating.)

How Would You Describe the Assessment Process?

We can talk about Jenny. You already know that she was a child who was identified by reading level as "struggling." In my school that meant that I asked her to read specific "benchmark texts," and she couldn't read them. The administration collected the results of these readings/tests and decided which children are "struggling." In other words Jenny was on the school's list of "at-risk" children and got a letter home saying she was a possible holdover, and intervention services would be given to her. This was done in January, about a month earlier than in other years. So the administration put Jenny on the "at-risk" list, but I didn't see it that way because she was just learning English. That's why she couldn't read the benchmark texts, so I decided to make Jenny my "case-study" child. I do this every year with a child I need to work with more closely.

(Since Jenny did not attend a pre-K on NCLB time, she was spared the "struggling" label as a 4-year-old. It's hard not to contrast Jenny's "at-risk" situation with that of Alice, Luisa, and Miguel, who were able to spend at least a year learning the language[s] and routines of schooling. The label itself placed Jenny at risk; as researchers have shown, being retained has no good effects [Shepard, 1999].)

Where Do You Start?

I start by looking at my notes. I usually take quick notes while I work with children, not standing apart. Sometimes I'm able to take notes when children are working on their own. In Jenny's case, I would work with her and take notes at the same time. I also collected her work and then looked at it later. It wasn't until I looked at it month after month—probably after 2 months—that I could see Jenny needed work on vocabulary.

How Did You Figure Out What to Do Next?

Then I look at my teaching. It's a lot easier to tweak the curriculum, my plans for what I'm going to teach next, when it's for a small group or for the whole class. It's harder for one child. I wondered, what wasn't I doing that would help Jenny?

I kept conferring with her, talking with her one-on-one. Since we use Reading/Writing Workshop, I set my own goals for each time I confer. I have a checklist that matches Workshop goals, with a space for my notes. What I noticed with Jenny was that for a goal like "adding details" in writing, she had trouble. Even though she knew basic conventions of writing, she didn't know some words for everyday things. It sounds simple, but I was stuck. I wasn't able to help her write a piece readers could understand.

Who Helped You Take the Next Step?

Someone like my colleague next door—the intervention teacher—the Reading Recovery teacher (Clay, 1993). In my school she was like a resource teacher part of the time, "pushing in," coming into my room on a regular basis, one period a day, five times a week. (In a "pullout" program children leave their room to work with resource teachers.) I asked her to take a look at what I had—notes, work samples from Jenny. And she came in and watched me confer, or she watched the kid. She didn't always look at a writing piece. Sometimes her insights and feedback can happen after she sees the kid at work.

In Jenny's case, the Reading Recovery teacher said I needed to be more explicit when I conferred. She suggested I tell Jenny about vocabulary in a different way from other kids. I have such a hard time intervening when I'm conferring—but in not intervening, I wasn't getting at what she needed, and that was direct instruction.

(In Ms. Hong's school, the classroom teacher can choose the "intervention" that the administrators promised in the letter home to Jenny's parents. So what's notable here is that the intervention is layered and included the outsider working with both Ms. Hong and Jenny and Ms. Hong working with Jenny.)

What Did Direct Instruction Look Like?

I wish I had my notes. OK, it seems so simple now. There was this writing time where Jenny had talked about going to the store to get food. She told a short story: "We bought food, we ate it. Oh, my mom made it." She didn't or couldn't include in her story that that was her *dinner.* I said, "Oh, she made *dinner.*"

After she was taught the word *dinner,* she wrote it over and over again, making up a longer story and using invented spelling (see Figure 6.4). I don't remember writing any of the words for her. If I did, they would've been spelled correctly; she probably sounded them out. That's what they learned to do in the supplemental phonics program. She wanted to write a story about food—about having dinner with her family: "I went to the store and bought food for dinner. I bought cheese, milk, bread, and chicken. My mom made dinner, and we ate dinner" (her story conventionally spelled).

FIGURE 6.4. Jenny's "Dinnr" Story

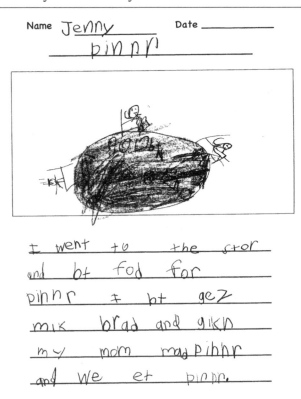

Did Jenny Continue to Learn Vocabulary in This Direct Way?

Yes, it started her learning vocabulary in English. She seemed to pick up a strategy—listen to me tell her a word, then repeat it orally and in writing, over and over. Looking back, I think she learned words in the most meaningful contexts. So *family*, for example—instead of naming every member of her family, she began to use the word *family*. And she started to write the word *we*, instead of listing every member of her family plus *I*.

Jenny continued to make progress, and by the end of the year, she was at level three, called "meeting expectations," in other words, "on level" for an almost 1st grader. I knew she could do it. She wasn't held over. She went to 1st grade in the fall, and she keeps in touch with me by writing letters.

(Ms. Hong is attentive to the particulars of how Jenny is using language in these workshop contexts. We agree emphatically that Ms. Hong's reasoning, explained in the next section, about Jenny, an EB, cannot be applied to another child, who may not be an EB and has a different constellation of resources and needs. For instance, when Mrs. Bee's Alicia wrote with her teacher, her written vocabulary was repetitive and limited but not because of a general problem with vocabulary learning [see Chapter 5]. Each child is a uniquely dynamic and complex character.)

How Do You Assess All Your Children?

Assessment in itself is challenging because it has to be done thoroughly. It helps that there are always goals in mind as I assess, so I'm not sitting with a child not knowing what to look for. Overall the process is equitable; that is, I see every child and group on a rotational basis. However, what's not equal is the actual time spent working with certain children. So some conferences take longer, and some kids need more help and follow-up. I know this might sound weird, but it's often easier to assess the children who are "struggling." Goal-setting for the next round is clearer.

The hardest group of children to assess, then to "differentiate" their instruction, is the one that "exceeds grade-level standards" (a term used by the New York City Department of Education). Two years ago, I had a girl, Carrie, who came in reading beyond the level of a "typical" kindergartner. At the end of the year, she read and comprehended at level L (benchmark level in 2nd grade), and her writing was that of a 1st grader. It was challenging trying to keep up with her. She was truly a sponge. For example, if I taught her to place periods at the end of her sentence or thought, rather than at the end of each line, she did it the next day. If I taught her how to make various connections to text while reading, she would listen, and then apply it—easily.

The most challenging aspect for Carrie was not so much the teaching part, but rather that she didn't have opportunities to explore learning with her peers.

Because her needs were so different from the other children's, she couldn't really be included in a group I would work with, like a guided reading (a small group of children at the same reading level) or strategy group (a small group of children who needed to learn the same strategy—e.g., punctuation at the ends of sentences). Reading and writing time became only academic tasks, things she did in school, rather than also a social event, which to me is incredibly important. So I had to seek help; I spoke with my colleague who taught in the kindergarten's gifted program. We created a guided reading group for my child and my colleague's kids, her "highest" readers. They came over three times a week during my reading workshop time. This was a change that needed to take place for this child. It allowed Carrie to see that reading is a social event and not something she just does at school. Oh, and she continued to thrive.

(We note the interesting "push in" choices that teachers can make at Ms. Hong's school, inviting people in rather than sending children out. Unlike Cohen's fictional Anna Maria in the 1st-grade classroom, Carrie was not sent down the hall to the gifted class. Instead "gifted" children came to her to orchestrate reading as a social event. We note as well that Ms. Hong's pedagogical concern echoed our own, voiced throughout this book, that written language be "relevant" to children's lives as children [Vygotsky, 1978, p. 118].)

How Would You Sum Up Your Ways of Assessing?

You have to have more than one way, because one way doesn't get to the heart of what we're looking for. For example, hand-written notes or anecdotes are valuable, but they are not always objective or complete. So I have five ways of assessing. We provide different modes of learning for kids, and I know that *what I do with Jenny might not work at all with someone else.* We do the same thing with assessing them—use different ways. It took me a long time to be able to work in assessment activities, and I don't use all of them every year. I'm still working on fitting them into my days. I want to make it all purposeful and authentic, not superficial. So here's the list of things I do when I teach kindergarten:

1. *Notes and anecdotes.* Often I take observational notes when I'm working with children; I might write them on the bottom of a checklist. Anecdotes are a little longer: what you see the kids doing, not usually when you're interacting with them. I think of these as partial portraits— you move on after you write an anecdote; but in your head there's a "to be continued" sign because you're in a roomful of children. You'll come back to the anecdote or have a chance later to reflect on it.
2. *Checklists.* These outline or break down some aspect of children's literacy learning and show things a beginning writer can do (see Figure 6.5.) I create the list and illustrate it, and children check off the things they can do.

3. *Commercially published curriculum tests.* The year that Jenny was in my class we used Fundations (2005). It's mandated (and approved by Reading First) and all about phonics, so I adapt it. At the end of each unit there's a test; and that's all there is. So I take the test data and put it on a class grid. I use the test's category or skill, but then I put my own box next to it regarding what the student needs to work on.
4. *Portfolio.* This is a collection of children's work over time. It has examples of all the other forms of assessment, plus samples of their work from other areas like art or social studies.
5. *Videotapes and audiotapes.* These go beyond anecdotes because they are more complete, less biased records. Interpreting them is critical and eye-opening because they make me see things that I don't want to see sometimes. Transcribing tapes, though, is very time-consuming, so I'm not able to do taping every year.

Figure 6.5 Ms. Hong's Writing Checklist as Completed by Jenny

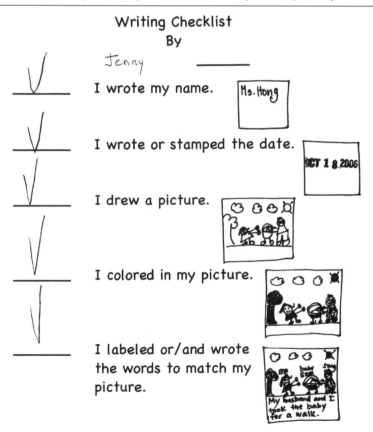

That list probably seems long. So my advice to teachers who are just beginning to assess their children is to jump in and do what you can. If you have questions, don't be afraid to find someone outside your classroom who can look at what you're doing with you. Then you'll see things that you didn't think you could. Mainly, don't be afraid to ask!

In this straightforward interview Ms. Hong weaves in examples of her assessment practices and rationale for them, within a particular public school context. How her perspective and practices fit into the range of issues offered in this chapter is addressed next.

ASSESSING CHILDREN'S LANGUAGE AND LITERACY: IT'S NEVER SIMPLE

We began this chapter feeling anxious for the storied 1st graders and their race to the finish of a standardized test. And we noted that in these eclectic, fluid, and sometimes contradictory, postmodern times, teachers have to become multitemporal thinkers as early as their students' kindergarten year. In the primary grades of many schools, teachers are now required to use a specific curriculum, give homework, and pay attention to NCLB or panoptical time and the tests that mark it, at the same time that they feel obligated to work on a parallel path with children like Jenny with diverse inner clocks. Thus, despite what Ms. Hong said about her "simple" definition of assessment, the process is never simple. It may look simple only after the intense work of observing/documenting/assessing is done.

Ms. Hong used the word *simple* again as she described the challenge of teaching Jenny English vocabulary. Yet the way to address the challenge involved the school's Reading Recovery teacher and collaboration over time. Similarly, at SYC Joanne found herself on a nonlinear, complex assessment time line with Allan, whose diagnosis of PDD-NOS initiated a series of parental choices that were communicated to the staff at SYC. In her comments introducing Joanne's story, Jan revealed that her and her colleagues' attitude toward such diagnoses in the pre-K years had changed. Indeed the times have changed as more children are found to be on the autism spectrum, and interventions at speech and hearing clinics may help children like Allan to communicate, over unhurried time to begin to be sociolinguistically flexible. Since this broad communicative goal prevails in some classrooms, you are able to see how two assessment time lines, Allan's and Jenny's, develop concretely through complex stories of individuals learning.

Changing Views of "Intervention": Their Relationship to Theory

In divergent settings both Jan and Ms. Hong refer to the need for *intervention*. In Jan's case, she refers to greater acceptance of the diagnoses of specialists who may work with children like Allan in ways that are highly structured and repetitive as they teach him to communicate (Hyman & Towbin, 2007). This form of intervention, direct instruction, has been discouraged in "general education" classrooms for pre-kindergartners, at least within the framework of developmentally appropriate practice (Bredekamp & Copple, 1997), since it has such a different feel and impact from Jan's more typical "intervention" or friendly suggestion during Dominic and friends' boisterous hockey game. Similarly, Ms. Hong's preference is to be indirect, not to "intervene" while conferring. In contrast, her Reading Recovery colleague advised her to try direct instruction with kindergartner Jenny, an EB.

We see in Allan's and Jenny's stories support for and challenges to "universal" assumptions about language learning, which we emphasized in Chapters 2 and 3. As a reminder, we asserted:

1. Almost all persons learn their primary or home language by virtue of being human, not through direct instruction by adults.
2. Children learn language, on whatever path at whatever rate, on a social plane. Language learning comes through countless interactions with others across varied sociocultural contexts.
3. Language exists in dialogue with others in a sociolinguistically complex world. Something articulated—said or written—is an invitation for response from others.

Despite their need to learn particular language forms and sociolinguistic practices, according to their teachers, both Allan and Jenny sought to socialize with classroom peers. Thus, their behavior and apparent desires were in keeping with the second and third assertions; they attempted to be in dialogue with others in varied sociocultural contexts.

By his 3rd year of life, however, Allan was not among the group we refer to in the first assertion as "almost all persons." For whatever reason, greater numbers of very young children are not learning to communicate or use their home language without some form of intervention. (Indeed, clinicians' expanding the list of criteria for children with ASD in the revised *Diagnostic and Statistical Manual IV* [American Psychiatric Association, 2000] may itself have led to identifying more children with related disorders.) Through Joanne's story we learn that the norm reflected in our assertion about persons *in general* learning language without instruction can easily dominate our ways of thinking about individual children's development. This dominance makes it difficult for parents, who understandably see their children as "perfect," or for teachers or researchers to accept the need for early intervention. (For a contrasting, noninterventionist parent's approach with "late-talking children," though, see Sowell, 1997.)

In a different sociocultural context Jenny, an EB or ELL, presumably learned Spanish, her primary or home language, without intervention. Yet in the classroom, Ms. Hong needed to deviate from her own pedagogical norms and diversify her teaching strategies to include direct instruction for Jenny. Again this solution seems deceptively "simple," but only in retrospect, as it evolved over time in a complex social and educational network. Ms. Hong's enacted definition of "direct instruction" differs from the usual one, which calls to mind an image of teachers following a script with a group of children who learn by rote (Bereiter & Engelmann, 1966). In contrast, Ms. Hong is using the term to describe providing specific information to Jenny, whom she judges to need the information in the conversational context of conferring. In that context, Ms. Hong sees how explicit vocabulary information—a word like *dinner*—would help the child further her communicative intention and, because of that, she is likely to appropriate the vocabulary. Moreover, the instructional context allows the child time and space to take control of the word in a comfortable way. Assessments of different kinds from different sources, coupled with to-the-point yet complex curricular changes in particular contexts, underlay both Joanne's and Ms. Hong's movement toward a more inclusive, expansive, and productive curriculum.

Flexible Maneuvering in Changing Times

Like anything related to language and literacy, assessment time lines for individual children do not follow a straight line. Thus, in this chapter we have stressed the untidy lines, whose shapes are seen only in retrospect. Joanne and Ms. Hong worried over the apparent flatness of Allan's and Jenny's time lines, with respect to particular communicative goals, until changes in pedagogy led to steps toward greater sociolinguistic flexibility. These steps leading upward and outward depended as much on the children's responses and actions as on adults' pedagogical decisions.

Perhaps an insight to be drawn is that to be truly "child-centered" we sometimes adapt practices that we once found objectionable and resisted. At the same time, we remind ourselves that approaches and practices we choose for one child may be resisted or inappropriate and thus wholly ineffective for another. Finally, we remind ourselves that diagnoses of "disorder" and recommendations for "intervention" are socially constructed in very particular social, educational, and historical contexts of which we must be continually aware.

In our concluding chapter we return to the underlying themes of this book, and we turn to what teachers do and can do in these diverse times as they support young children's learning of language and literacy. Like us, teachers aim to develop children's sociolinguistic flexibility so that they can step outward to participate in expanding social and academic worlds.

7. Children with Teachers
Looking Back and Moving Forward

The esteemed children's author Eloise Greenfield and her mother Lessie Jones Little introduce their book, *Childtimes: A Three-Generation Memoir,* in this way:

> People are part of their time. They are affected, during the time that they live, by the things that happen in their world. Big things and small things. A war, an invention such as radio or television, a birthday party, a kiss. All of these experiences help to shape people, and they, in turn, help to shape the present and the future. . . . This book is about . . . children and their times, the times in which they grew up. It's about how those times were similar and how they were different. (Greenfield & Little, 1979, n.p.)

In the book, Greenfield and Little's childhoods, and that of Greenfield's grandmother, are captured in memories undeniably shaped by forces of race, socioeconomic class, technology, geography and, of course, history. But the very language of those memories evokes not broad portraits of troubled times, but particular worlds of important relationships, everyday pleasures and struggles, and always play winding itself around work, school, and church.

In our book we, too, have visited "childtimes," children enacting the spaces and times of their lives, taking their place "in this procession of children" (Greenfield & Little, 1979, n.p.). The children we have featured are each unique, situated in very specific ways within societal structures, classroom contexts, and everyday relations. But still, there are themes that link the children and their teachers in this book, itself written in response to our own times. These themes are woven throughout our efforts to problematize curricular uniformity and to normalize childhood diversity.

In this chapter our purpose is to summarize and elaborate upon key themes, which illustrate in particular school settings the ways in which teachers work with children in today's diverse times. We address the following topics:

- Curricular and sociolinguistic flexibility
- Multitemporality and flexible classroom clocks
- Play as the essence of flexible curricula in inflexible times, and
- A future when diversity is the norm.

The last topic incorporates advocating for more child-worthy practices, as we point toward a future of challenge and action.

CURRICULAR AND SOCIOLINGUISTIC FLEXIBILITY

Recall that in Chapter 1 we described the puzzling and awesome disconnect between the flourishing diversity of children and their families and the uniformity of curricula that is offered in many schools. However, what we call NCLB, or panoptical, time affects teachers and their children differently. The Head Start and SYC teachers' curricula are philosophically opposed to the narrow guidelines underlying NCLB time and the tests that regularly segment it. These pre-K teachers provide curricular activities that are open to children with distinctive inner clocks, linguistic and socioeconomic backgrounds, and ways of engaging others. Further, within the stories that children enact as part of their expanding social relationships, teachers persistently seek connections between classroom activity and children's interests and abilities.

Teachers work with children, like Dominic and Tommy, whose energies and interests put them immediately on a sociable path to action and talk, and with observant but not passive children like Alice or Luisa on a quieter path nearby. In time we saw Alice and Luisa manipulating the symbols of spoken and written languages in contexts that were inseparable from their relationships with friends. Indeed, it was in these contexts where we first glimpsed evidence of their sociolinguistic flexibility. Their teachers persisted in maintaining their flexible curricula despite pressures to make them more academic, a point we will return to in the last section of this chapter.

Beginning in kindergarten, there is often a stark curricular shift. Because of the prescribed literacy-focused curricula that many schools or districts require, teachers need an even higher level of persistence and resistance. These teachers and their children are less able to avoid the pressures of NCLB time and feel coveted opportunities for childtimes slip away. Unlike children in some preschools, primary grade children may experience a clear separation between the official world and unofficial, child-constructed worlds.

Yet Mrs. Kay provided time and space for a lively child culture to develop, sustained by friendship and the pleasures of play. As Tionna and her peers illustrated, this "unofficial world" infused new meanings into the official world which, in turn, provided the children with resources for new kinds of play and new ways of using oral and written language. Indeed, throughout the book we introduced you to classrooms where in diverse ways, over time, teachers appreciated and, moreover, negotiated connections to children's existing and developing abilities and interests. In this way a productive interplay between child and teacher agendas could gradually unfold. We view this interplay as fundamental to teachers' ability to know their children and, moreover, to promote children's flexibility and adaptability as language learners.

MULTITEMPORALITY AND FLEXIBLE CLASSROOM CLOCKS

The children you have met in the preceding chapters demonstrated that time lines vary widely, within and across individual children. And only some of the children experienced unhurried time, what we see as a necessary element of childtimes. Like Cohen's (1980/2006) 1st-grade teacher, Eloise Greenfield and Lessie Jones Little (1979) affirm with their lives the primacy of childtimes. They expand the meaning of multitemporal—or the ability to speed up and slow down time to adapt to varied situations—to include intergenerational time. The generations that knew pre-NCLB time remind us of how expansive everyday experiences can be. Thus, within a single classroom, young children's experience with a timed test is counterbalanced in Cohen's 1st-grade space by, for example, cookies made by the teacher and weighed by the children on an old-fashioned scale. At other times in other classroom spaces, children might play games that their teachers played in their childtimes, recite rhymes that have been passed through generations of children, as Tionna and her friends did with Mrs. Kay, sing songs that were written decades ago as Luisa did in Ms. de Luna's kindergarten, all alongside child-created dramas and stories of contemporary superheroes. So pre-kindergartners like Miguel in Chapter 3 became bilingual in unhurried time in classrooms where the "older generation" of teachers spoke the languages he was learning; and play, the possession of all generations, was not an option but a curricular staple. In the unhurried time of play-based curricula, pre-kindergartners like Alice, Luisa, and Miguel enacted their unique assessment time lines as their bilingual abilities added to their sociolinguistic flexibility. Like Allan, who showed "language delay," these children developed the language that mediated a gradual entry into the social worlds of their classrooms. Just as there was no uniformity in the time line of one child as compared with others, there was no rigid curricular uniformity to which their pre-K teachers had to adhere.

As we expressed throughout our book, early childhood settings like Allan's or the fictional 1st grade where children's broad-ranging abilities are on display are becoming rare—truly idyllic in the 21st-century—as is freedom from academic pressures. Further, the sense that family members and teachers are handing down knowledge accumulated in their play-filled childtimes is often invisible. Many children, like Alicia in Chapter 5, are expected to march to the beat of a paced curriculum, punctuated by frequent tests, especially tests about literacy.

But, as Alicia herself vividly illustrated, children do not learn written language according to the dictates of curriculum supervisors. In the official curriculum, or along a "curricular sideroad" (Dyson, 1993, p. 178), children need time and space to explore the complexities of the written system, to make personal connections with those rather dull-looking lines and curves, to ease into the rhyme and rhythm of matching voice and print, and most basic of all, to sense the relevance of written language as a communicative medium, a means to some end. Indeed, Alicia herself used some old childtime practices as she made sense of the new literacy demands—she told imaginative stories, she drew invented worlds, and she engaged in social play and collaborative problem-solving with her friends. We, too, have aimed to call attention to playful practices as central to children's sense of themselves as agents with some power in their worlds.

PLAY AS THE ESSENCE OF CURRICULA IN INFLEXIBLE TIMES: "I HAVE TO DO WHAT I THINK IS RIGHT"

So reasoned Mrs. Kay as she reflected on how she worked within and around the mandated literacy curriculum. She, like Ms. Hong in Chapter 6, took professional liberties within the mandated curriculum, based on what she thought would benefit children. Among these liberties was time for play.

For her part, Mrs. Kay felt that children needed opportunities for physical activity on the playground and for constructive and dramatic play in the classroom. So, around the mandated schedule of lessons, Mrs. Kay allowed such opportunities. As she observed, or worked one-to-one with a child needing help with editing a text or untangling a math problem, her children assumed responsibility for making activity choices. They could be heard talking about how to distribute weight to make a Lego car stable or to fashion an angled plane for racing those cars and, of course, they could be observed taking dramatic roles in imagined scenes they enacted.

Such play is not anti-academic. First, it provides rich opportunities for children to flexibly use language in a range of communicative events; after all, language is "child's play," as Momaday's Bear said (Momaday, 1999, p. 40; see Chapter 4). To play collaboratively, children not only have to express themselves to one another, but they have to adapt their language to the situation at hand. Remember the birthday party givers celebrating their teacher, the "cool dudes" admiring their "mean" cars, the in-charge mother keeping those boys in check, or the "teachers" authoritatively articulating a spelling test. This same ear for situated language accounts, in part at least, for children's capacity to try out new variants of language, including that regarded as "standard," and to appreciate the sociolinguistic dance of code-switching, when speakers move among languages.

Second, as stressed in Chapter 5, time to play not only benefits children's oral language, but it benefits written language as well. Teachers like Mrs. Kay, Ms. Hong, and Mrs. Bee provide materials, models, and interactively attuned guidance but, with one another, children may infuse childhood concerns and practices into literacy activities. In this way, children's unofficial world, and their often intense interest in one another, does not work against their official literacy learning, but rather for it. Mrs. Bee, for instance, sensitively demanded increasingly conventional writing from Alicia. But her first conventional word, other than Alicia, was Willo, the name of her play sister; and her "own" independent move into systematically encoded writing happened when she responded to a peer's correction by asserting her own competence. (Of course her "own" move happened with the assistance, however unacknowledged, of her peers.)

Given time and space, children may bring into the classroom kinds of literacy knowledge and know-how that are unanticipated by the curriculum. From graphic conventions (like dialogue bubbles and stop signs) to wholly new practices (like pop up cards), observant teachers can incorporate children's interests into the literacy curriculum, making it permeable to children's worlds. In all these ways, children from varied social and cultural backgrounds may form a communicatively complex, unofficial world that is intricately connected to the official one. The worlds are dynamically linked, each potentially enriched by the other. In fact, the value of play for children's language and literacy may account for Ms. Hong's curricular decisions in her kindergarten. She felt that she had to give up time for social studies and science because of the heavy demand for literacy, but she told us that she would not give up time for daily play in her kindergarten.

In addition to making space for play, we have also seen teachers deciding to make pedagogical choices that did not necessarily conform to the mandated language curriculum. Mrs. Bee in particular was grappling with how to do what she felt was right without in any way compromising her children's ability to perform on the mandated assessments. Unlike Ms. Hong and Mrs. Kay, Mrs. Bee was new to her grade level, with its academic pressure; she felt rushed by the paced kindergarten curriculum and the looming assessments of her children's reading and writing. Mrs. Bee felt her children could achieve the mandated goals—and they did—but "whether or not they should, that's another story," she said. She wanted her children to have more opportunities to carry on conversations, to express their points of view, to assume character roles, to appropriate taught concepts into dramatic play. So she was making plans, trying to maneuver more room for children and for herself.

TOWARD A FUTURE WHEN DIVERSITY IS THE NORM

> This has been the century of strangers, brown, yellow, and white. This has been the century of the great immigrant experiment. It is only this late in the day that you can walk into a playground and find Isaac Leung by the fish pond, Danny Rahman in the football cage, Quang O'Rourke bouncing a basketball, and Irie Jones humming a tune. Children with first and last names on a direct collision course.
>
> —Zadie Smith (2000, p. 271)

From a unique angle, in a distinctive voice, Zadie Smith looks back toward 20th-century London and celebrates a century of strangers in her novel *White Teeth*. Through this complex and vibrant story she captures the eclectic, multiethnic, fluid, and edgy qualities—the postmodern diversity—of contemporary social worlds in London and around the globe. In this section we focus on ways of supporting in the wide and public arena of education the premise that the ethnically and socioeconomically diverse persons who fill Smith's novel can no longer be called strangers because "diversity is the new normal."

Research as Support for Diversity

We first look back at research that has revealed that the "strangers" in our classrooms who may or may not be newcomers to the United States are not really strangers at all, but instead the soul of the increasingly diverse social worlds that constitute our classrooms. Indeed, the research we ourselves have engaged in attempts to capture sociolinguistic aspects of that soul. And if there is a "collision course," it seems not to be between boundary-crossing first and last names, but between young children of every background and the uniform curricula that leave no space for them—children with unique abilities, strengths, weaknesses, agendas, and of course inner clocks.

We include here a few studies and collections of studies that were not cited earlier, but move across our key themes and undergird our premise that "diversity is the new normal." Their inclusion does not mean that we can articulate here or agree with their myriad findings; rather, it means that the cited researchers push us to look at language, literacy, and children with their teachers in complex and expansive ways. Becoming familiar with the breadth of research prepares us to support more substantively our own theories and practices.

Two reports that focus on "language-minority" children are *Improving Schooling for Language-Minority Children* (August & Hakuta, 1997) and *Developing Literacy in Second-Language Learners* (August & Shanahan, 2006). Both incorporate extensive reviews of literature, and both conclude with the overall recommendation with which we agree: *to maintain English learners' home languages through, for example, bilingual education programs, while they learn spoken and written English.* Because the government agency that funded the report on developing literacy (August & Shanahan, 2006) disagreed strongly with this recommendation, the report was highly politicized before it was published by a commercial press, rather than by the government agency (see Grant, Wong, & Osterling, 2007, for a critical review). Our view is that the mostly large-scale research reported in both volumes leans too far in the direction of homogenizing literacy curricula for children labeled "at risk" and characterized by what they cannot do. Still, we should be knowledgeable about the content of the reports so that we can talk back to their inaccurate or narrow representations of children, teachers, language, and literacy.

In a more positive vein, there are recent publications that support the inclusion of play in early childhood classrooms. In particular, the edited collection called *Play = Learning* (Singer, Golinkoff, & Hirsh-Pasek, 2006) includes research-based chapters that address varied topics like recess, science, self-regulation, autism, technology, and early literacy. We have already cited Paley's book (2004) on the importance of fantasy play, and you may be familiar with Elkind's (2007) *The Power of Play.* Similar in some ways to Paley's work, Elkind bases his arguments for play on his own experiences and clinical work with children. Thus, theirs are persuasive examples of practitioner research.

Finally, the topic of assessment is addressed by many researchers, some previously cited in Chapter 6 in the context of NCLB. We emphasize here work by Shepard (2006), whose goals link to those of teachers you met earlier. Shepard's focus is not on "linguistic minority" or play-deprived children, but on all learners who would be better served by classroom-based or *formative assessment.* This is not a new term (Bloom, Hastings, & Madaus, 1971), and it is sometimes used as a synonym for "alternative" or nonstandardized ways of assessing. Shepard's use of the term, however, is broader in that she attempts to systematize, across many classrooms, ways of assessing what teachers and learners do day-to-day in classrooms.

She concisely states, "For teachers to be effective in supporting student learning, they must constantly be checking for student understanding" (Shepard, 2006, p. 627). This kind of "checking" is enacted in the moment-

tion, note-taking, questioning, scaffolding, and talking that teachers you met
in previous chapters needed unhurried time to accomplish. Not surprisingly,
according to Shepard (2006), the theoretical framework for this kind of assessment is Vygotskian: learning happens first on a social plane, and it is the teacher
who continually assesses where that moving plane might be so that children
learn most readily, a point we have made repeatedly. It is through social interactions like these that we hope learners, at first relative strangers to the teacher,
begin to enter the official world of language and literacy learning while never
abandoning their own playful, unofficial worlds.

In the final section on advocacy for practices that make child-sense, we keep
a focus on the importance of social relationships, most particularly among children, teachers, and the general public.

Advocating for Flexible Practices and Childtimes

> Well—our stories are told. . . . Now it's time for us to look forward
> again, to see where it is that we're going. . . . A childtime is a
> mighty thing.
>
> —Eloise Greenfield and Lessie Jones Little (1979, n. p.)

Eloise Greenfield and Lessie Jones Little lead us into our closing section,
urging us to look forward, now that our stories are told. What we see as we look
forward is a need to change the current story line in many early childhood classrooms so that practices become unhurried, flexible, and child-worthy. Through
the stories of children like pre-kindergartners Luisa and Allan, we have argued for
unhurried time and a respect for children's inner clocks.

Further, with regard to flexible curricula, we hope that many teachers will
critically consider the sense of curricular mandates. At varied points in this book,
we have worried about mandates that are linguistically unsound. For example,
there are curricular benchmarks that expect grammatical "correctness" from 5-
and 6-year-olds, with no acknowledgment of the diverse Englishes spoken by our
children, not to mention the many children just starting to learn English, and no
evident insight into how children become flexible communicators. There may
even be the assumption that repetition and sequential mastery of grammatical
forms are key aspects of language development (see California curriculum guidelines in Chapter 2).

Following on the need for flexible curricula to support children's sociolinguistic flexibility, we move on to highlight again and advocate for what we have
called the possession of all children: play. We have said in multiple places and in

multiple ways that regardless of the press of the official curriculum, children will find spaces for play. And because this is so, play spills into the processes of learning language and literacy and becomes the inevitable ingredient of child-worthy curriculum.

In sum, as we have explored what it means to embrace the normalcy of difference, we close by urging you to continue to problematize with us the uniform curricula on a collision course with the diverse ways in which children draw upon and learn the forms and uses of languages and literacy. And so as we look forward, we suggest that in our social and political relationships with one another we advocate for a number of goals, not limited to but including the following:

1. Unhurried time so that children in contemporary classrooms have possibilities to form vivid memories of childtimes
2. Practices that are worth taking time with, whether these are the core of a curriculum or "inserts" squeezed in and around less flexible mandated curricula
3. Access in pre- and in-service professional education courses to current information about language development and language variation so that teachers can begin to understand that diversity is the norm
4. Play by making it a "standard" in early childhood classrooms.

Advocacy is possible when people join language together with action—when they develop socially and politically focused "language-and-action" ways, which Lindfors (1999) described for children. There are countless activist groups that work to reform and transform educational policies and practices. Here are three, based in the United States, but accessible online and increasingly relevant to the education of young children:

- *Educatorroundtable.org*—The Educator Roundtable. This extensive online organization mobilized around inequities in No Child Left Behind legislation, with the aim of improving future post-NCLB legislation.
- *Fairtest.org*—The National Center for Fair and Open Testing (FairTest). Its purpose has been to end the misuse of standardized testing through advocacy and focused publications.
- *Rethinkingschools.org*—Rethinking Schools. This is a nonprofit publisher that focuses on issues of equity/inequity as they relate to the continual reform of elementary and secondary education.

Our hope is that through educators' persistent, child-worthy efforts in classrooms and the larger public arena, we can look toward a future where children and teachers can work and play with less pressure and greater flexibility, where we are able to find playgrounds full of children with names as diverse as their stories.

We hope, too, that through this book, we have succeeded in illustrating, discussing, appreciating—yes, even celebrating—the language-making genius of children and the pedagogical wisdom of teachers who observe, respond to, and grow with their children. In the dynamic interplay of child genius and teacher wisdom may be found the (play)grounds for language-rich classrooms worthy of our society's children—children of diverse times.

References

Adger, C. T., & Wolfram, W. (2000). Demythologizing the home-school language dichotomy: Sociolinguistic reality and instructional practice. In J. K. Peyton, P. Griffin, W. Wolfram & R. Rasold (Eds.), *Language in action: New studies of language in society* (pp. 391–407). Cresskill, NJ: Hampton Press.

Allington, R. (2002). *Big brother and the national reading curriculum: How ideology trumped evidence.* Portsmouth, NH: Heinemann.

Almy, M. C., & Genishi, C. (1979). *Ways of studying children: An observation manual for early childhood teachers.* New York: Teachers College Press.

Andersen, E. S. (1990). *Speaking with style: The sociolinguistic skills of children.* New York: Routledge.

American Academy of Pediatrics. (2006, October 9). *The importance of play in promoting healthy child development and maintaining strong parent-child bonds.* Elk Grove Village, IL: K. R. Ginsburg & the Committee on Communications and the Committee on Psychosocial Aspects of Child and Family Health. Available at *www.aap.org/pressroom/playFINAL.pdf.*

American Psychiatric Association (2000). *Diagnostic and Statistical Manual of Mental Disorders DSM-IV-TR* (4th ed.). Arlington, VA: American Psychiatric Publishing.

Ashton-Warner, S. (1963). *Teacher.* New York: Simon & Schuster.

August, D., & Hakuta, K. (Eds.). (1997). *Improving schooling for language-minority children: A research agenda.* Washington, DC: National Research Council, National Academy Press.

August, D., & Shanahan, T. (Eds.). (2006). *Developing literacy in second-language learners: Report of the National Literacy Panel on language-minority children and youth.* Mahwah, NJ: Erlbaum.

Bailey, R. (2004). American English: Its origins and history. In E. Finegan & J. R. Rickford (Eds.), *Language in the USA: Themes for the twenty-first century* (pp. 3–17). New York: Cambridge University Press.

Bakhtin, M. (1981). Discourse in the novel. In C. Emerson & M. Holquist (Eds.), *The dialogic imagination: Four essays by M. Bakhtin* (pp. 254–422). Austin: University of Texas Press.

Bakhtin, M. (1986). *Speech genres and other late essays.* Austin: University of Texas Press.

Ballenger, C. (1999). *Teaching other people's children: Literacy and learning in a bilingual classroom.* New York: Teachers College Press.

Baratz, S. A., & Baratz, J. C. (1970). Early childhood education: The social science base of institutional racism. *Harvard Educational Review 40*(1), 19–50.

Barkley, R. A., Koplowitz, S., Anderson, T., & McMurray, M. B. (1997). Sense of time in children with ADHD: Effects of duration distraction and stimulant medication. *Journal of the International Neuropsychological Society, 3*(4), 359–369.

Barton, D., & Hamilton, M. (1998). *Local literacies: Reading and writing in one community.* London: Routledge.

Bateson, G. (1956). The message "this is play." In B. Schaffner (Ed.), *Group processes* (pp. 145–242). New York: Macy.

Bauman, R. (1992). *Folklore, cultural performances, and popular entertainments: A communications-centered handbook.* New York: Oxford University Press.

147

Bereiter, C., & Engelmann, S. (1966). *Teaching disadvantaged children in the preschool.* Engle-wood Cliffs, NJ: Prentice-Hall.

Beresin, A. R. (1995). Double dutch and double cameras: Studying the transmission of culture in an urban school yard. In B. Sutton-Smith, J. Mechling, T. W. Johnson & F. R. McMahon (Eds.), *Children's folklore: A source book* (pp. 75–92). New York: Garland Publishing.

Bergen, D. (2006). Reconciling play and assessment standards: How to leave no child behind. In D. P. Fromberg & D. Bergen (Eds.), *Play from birth to twelve: Contexts, perspectives, and meanings* (2nd ed., pp. 233–240). New York: Routledge.

Blom, J. P., & Gumperz, J. J. (1986). Social meaning in linguistic structures: Code-switching in Norway. In J. J. Gumperz & D. Hymes (Eds.), *Directions in sociolinguistics: The ethnography of communication* (pp. 407–434). New York: Basil Blackwell.

Bloom, B. S., Hastings, T., & Madaus, G. F. (1971). *Handbook on formative and summative evaluation of student learning.* New York: McGraw-Hill.

Boulware, G. L., Schwartz, I. S., Sandall, S. R., & McBride, B. J. (2006). Project DATA for toddlers: An inclusive approach to very young children with autism spectrum disorder. *Topics in Early Childhood Special Education, 26*(2), 94–105.

Boyd, D., Grossman, P., Lankford, H., Loeb, S., & Wyckoff, J. (2008, May). *Who leaves? Teacher attrition and student achievement.* National Bureau of Economic Research (NBER), Working Paper No. 14022.

Bredekamp, S., & Copple, C. (1997). *Developmentally appropriate practice in early childhood programs* (Rev. ed.). Washington, DC: National Association for the Education of Young Children.

Bredekamp, S., & Shepard, L. (1989). How best to protect children from inappropriate school expectations, practices, and policies. *Young Children, 44*(3), 14–24.

Brody, J. E. (2007, April 3). A classroom of monkey bars and slides. *The New York Times,* D9.

Brown, M. W., & Hurd, C. (1947). *Goodnight moon.* New York: HarperCollins.

Brown, R. (1973). *A first language: The early stages.* Cambridge, MA: Harvard University Press.

Bruner, J. (1983). *Child's talk: Learning to use language.* New York: W. W. Norton & Company.

Bruner, J., & Haste, H. (1987). *Making sense: the child's construction of the world.* New York: Methuen.

Bryant, P. E., Bradley, L., MacLean, M., & Crossland, J. (1989). Nursery rhymes, phonological skills, and reading. *Journal of Child Language, 16,* 407–428.

Bull, T. (1990). Teaching school beginners to read and write in the vernacular. In E. H. Jahr & O. Lorentz (Eds.), *Tromso Linguistics in the Eighties.* Olso, Norway: Novus Press.

Bumiller, E. (2003, July 8). Bush seeks big changes in Head Start, drawing criticism from program's supporters. *New York Times Archives. http://query.nytimes.com/gst/fullpage.html?res=9B00E3D6143DF93BA35754C0A9659C8B63&scp=1&sq=e.%20bumiller%20july%20 8,%202003%20head%20start&st=cse* Retrieved October 13, 2008.

Cadwell, L. B., & Rinaldi, C. (2003). *Bringing learning to life: The Reggio approach to early childhood education* (2nd ed.). New York: Teachers College Press.

California State Department of Education (2007). *Reading/language arts framework for California public schools.* Sacramento, CA: California Department of Education Press.

Calkins, L. M. (2003). *Units of study for primary writing: A yearlong curriculum.* Portsmouth, NH: FirstHand.

Campbell, S., & Smith, K. (2001). Equity observation and images of fairness in childhood. In S. Grieshaber & G. S. Cannella (Eds.), *Embracing identities in early childhood education: Diversity and possibilities* (pp. 89–102). New York: Teachers College Press.

Casper, V., & Theilheimer, R. (Eds.). (in press). *Learning together: An introduction to early childhood education.* New York: McGraw-Hill.

Cazden, C. B. (1970). The neglected situation in child research and education. In F. Williams (Ed.), *Language and poverty: Perspectives on a theme* (pp. 81–101). Chicago: Markham.

Cazden, C. (2001). *Classroom discourse: The language of teaching and learning.* Portsmouth, NH: Heinemann.

Cazden, C., Cordeiro, P., & Giacobbe, M. E. (1992). Spontaneous and scientific concepts: Learning punctuation in the first grade. In C. Cazden (Ed.), *Whole language plus: Essays on literacy in the United States and New Zealand* (pp. 81–98). New York: Teachers College.

Chittenden, E., Salinger, T., with Bussis, A. (2001). *Inquiry into meaning: An investigation of learning to read* (Rev. ed.). New York: Teachers College Press.

Chomsky, C. (1969). *The acquisition of syntax in children from 5 to 10.* Cambridge, MA: MIT Press.

Chomsky, N. (1965). *Aspects of the theory of syntax.* Cambridge, MA: M.I.T. Press.

Chomsky, N. (1968). *Language and mind.* New York: Harcourt.

Chrismer, S. S., Hodge, S. T, & Saintil, D. (Eds.). (2006). Assessing NCLB: Perspectives and prescriptions. *Harvard Educational Review* (special issue), *76*(4).

Cisneros, S. (1997). *Hairs.* Albuquerque, NM: Dragonfly Books.

Clark, E. V. (2003). *First language acquisition.* Cambridge, MA: Cambridge University Press.

Clay, M. M. (1975). *What did I write?* Auckland, New Zealand: Heinemann.

Clay, M. M. (1977). Exploring with a pencil. *Theory into Practice, 16,* 334–41.

Clay, M. M. (1993). *Reading Recovery: A guidebook for teachers in training.* Auckland, New Zealand: Heinemann.

Clay, M. M. (1998). *By different paths to common outcomes.* York, ME: Stenhouse.

Clifton, L. (1992). *Three wishes.* New York: Doubleday.

Cochran-Smith, M., & Lytle, S. (2006). Troubling images of teaching in No Child Left Behind. *Harvard Educational Review* (special issue), *76*(4), 668–697.

Cohen, D. H., Stern, V., Balaban, N., & Gropper, N. (2008). *Observing and recording the behavior of young children* (5th ed.). New York: Teachers College Press.

Cohen, M. (2006). *First grade takes a test* (rev. ed.). New York: Star Bright Books. (Original work published 1980)

Cohen, Y. A. (2000). The shaping of men's minds. In B. Levinson (Ed.), *Schooling the symbolic animal* (pp. 83–107). Lanham, MD: Rowman & Littlefield. (Original work published 1971)

Cole, M. (1986). Foreword. In V. G. Paley, *Mollie is three: Growing up in school* (pp. vii–xiii). Chicago: University of Chicago Press.

Comber, B., & Nixon, H. (2004). Children reread and rewrite their local neighborhoods: Critical literacies and identity work. In J. Evans (Ed.), *Literacy moves on: Using popular culture, new technologies and critical literacy in the primary classroom* (pp. 115–133). London: Fulton.

Corsaro, W. A. (2003). *"We're friends, right?": Inside kids' cultures.* Washington, DC: Joseph Henry Press.

Cosentino de Cohen, C., Deterding, N., & Clewell, B. C. (2005). *Who's left behind? Immigrant children in high and low LEP schools.* Washington, DC: The Urban Institute.

Cummins, J. (1979). *Cognitive/academic language proficiency, linguistic interdependence, the optimum age question, and some other matters. Working Papers on Bilingualism, 19,* 121–129.

Cummins, J. (2000). *Language, power, & pedagogy: Bilingual children caught in the cross-fire.* Clevedon, United Kingdom: Multilingual Matters.

Delpit, L. (1998). What should teachers do: Ebonics and culturally responsive instruction. In T. Perry & L. Delpit (Eds.), *The real Ebonics debate: Power, language, and the education of African American children* (pp. 17–26). Boston: Beacon Press.

Delpit, L. (2003). Educators as "seed people" growing a new future. *Educational Researcher, 32,* 14–21.

Delpit, L. D., & Dowdy, J. K. (Eds.).(2002). *The skin that we speak: Thoughts on language and culture in the classroom.* New York: New Press.

Derman-Sparks, L., & Anti-Bias Curriculum Task Force (Calif.) (1989). *Anti-bias curriculum: Tools for empowering young children.* Washington, DC: National Association for the Education of Young Children.

Dyson, A. Haas. (1982). The emergence of visible language: Interrelationships between drawing and early writing. *Visible Language, 16,* 360–381.

Dyson, A. Haas. (1987). Individual differences in beginning composing: An orchestral vision of learning to write. *Written Communication, 4*(4), 411–442.

Dyson, A. Haas. (1989). *Multiple worlds of child writers: Friends learning to write.* New York: Teachers College Press.

Dyson, A. Haas. (1993). *Social worlds of children learning to write in an urban primary school.* New York: Teachers College Press.

Dyson, A. Haas. (1997). *Writing superheroes: Contemporary childhood, popular culture, and classroom literacy.* New York: Teachers College Press.

Dyson, A. Haas. (1999). Transforming transfer: Unruly children, contrary texts, and the persistence of the pedagogical order. In A. Iran-Nejad & P. D. Pearson (Eds.), *Review of research in education: Vol. 24.* Washington, DC: American Educational Research Association.

Dyson, A. Haas. (2003). *The brothers and sisters learn to write: Popular literacies in childhood and school cultures.* New York: Teachers College Press.

Dyson, A. Haas. (2006). On saying it right (write): "Fix-its" in the foundations of learning to write. *Research in the Teaching of English, 41,* 8–44.

Dyson, A. Haas. (2007). School literacy and the development of a child culture: Written remnants of the "gusto of life." In D. Thiessen & A. Cook-Sather (Eds.), *International handbook of student experiences in elementary and secondary school* (pp. 115–142). Dordrecht, The Netherlands: Kluwer.

Dyson, A. Haas. (2008a). On listening to child composers: Beyond "fix-its." In C. Genishi & A. L. Goodwin (Eds.), *Diversities in early childhood education: Rethinking and doing* (pp. 13–28). New York: Routledge.

Dyson, A. Haas. (2008b). Research Directions, The Pine Cone Wars: Studying writing in a community of children. *Language Arts, 85,* 305–316.

Dyson, A. Haas, & Smitherman, G. (in press). The right (write) start: African American Language and the discourse of sounding right. *Teachers College Record.*

Early Reading First. (2002). *Guide to U.S. Department of Education Programs.* Retrieved July 5, 2007: *http://www.ed.gov/programs/earlyreading/index.html*

Elementary and Secondary Education Act of 1965. Retrieved October 5, 2008, from: *http://wps.prenhall.com/wps/media/objects/2355/2412111/Documents_Library/esea1965.htm*

Elkind, D. (2007). *The power of play: Learning what comes naturally.* Philadelphia, PA: DaCapo/Perseus.

Engelmann, S., Haddox, P., & Bruner, E. (1983). *Teach your child to read in 100 easy lessons.* New York: Simon & Schuster.

Erickson, F. (2007). Culture in society and in educational practices. In J. Banks & C. A. M. Banks (Eds.), *Multicultural education: Issues and perspectives* (2nd ed., pp. 33–57). Hoboken, NJ: Wiley.

Fassler, R. (2003). *Room for talk: Teaching and learning in a multilingual kindergarten.* New York: Teachers College Press.

Ferreiro, E., & Teberosky, A. (1982). *Literacy before schooling.* Exeter, NH: Heinemann.

Fountas, I. C., & Pinnell, G. S. (1996). *Guided reading: Good first teaching for all children.* Portsmouth, NH: Heinemann.

Franklin, M. B. (1983). Play as the creation of imaginary situations: The role of language. In S. Wapner & B. Kaplan (Eds.), *Toward a holistic developmental psychology* (pp. 197–220). Hillsdale, NJ: Erlbaum.

Gallas, K. (1992). When children take the chair: A study of sharing time in a primary classroom. *Language Arts, 69,* 172–182.

Garan, E. M. (2004). *In defense of our children: When politics, profit, and education collide.* Portsmouth, NH: Heinemann.

García, E. E. (2005). *Teaching and learning in two languages: Bilingualism and schooling in the United States.* New York: Teachers College Press.

Garcia, O., Kleifgen, J., & Falchi, L. (2008). *From English language learners to emergent bilinguals.* Equity Matters: Research Review No. 1. *http://www.tc.columbia.edu/i/a/document/6468_Ofelia_ELL__Final.pdf*

Garvey, C. (1984). *Children's talk.* Cambridge, MA: Harvard University Press.

Garvey, C. (1990). *Play* (enl. ed.). Cambridge, MA: Harvard University Press.

Genishi, C. (Ed.). (1992). *Ways of assessing children and curriculum: Stories of early childhood practice.* New York: Teachers College Press.

Genishi, C. (2002). Young English language learners: Resourceful in the classroom. *Young Children, 57*(4), 66–72.

Genishi, C., & Dyson, A. H. (1984). *Language assessment in the early years.* Norwood, NJ: Ablex.

Genishi, C., Stires, S., & Yung-Chan, D. (2001). Writing in an integrated curriculum: Prekindergarten English language learners as symbol makers. In A. H. Dyson (Ed.), *Elementary School Journal* (special issue) *101*(4), 399–416.

Genishi, C., Yung-Chan, D., & Stires, S. (2000). Talking their way into print: English language learners in a prekindergarten classroom. In D. S. Strickland & L. M. Morrow (Eds.), *Beginning reading and writing* (pp. 66–80). New York: Teachers College Press.

Gillen, J. (2002). Moves in the territory of literacy: The telephone discourse of three- and four-year olds. *Journal of Early Childhood Literacy, 2,* 21–43.

Gilliam, J. E. (2006). *Gilliam Autism Rating Scale* (GARS-2, 2nd ed.). Bloomington, MN: Pearson Education.

Gilmore, P. (1985). "Gimme room": School resistance, attitude and access to literacy. *Journal of Education, 167,* 111–127.

Gleick, J. (1999). *Faster: The accelerating of just about everything.* New York: Vintage.

Glupczynski, T. (2007). *Understanding young children's experiences with a scripted literacy curriculum.* Unpublished dissertation, Teachers College, New York.

Godley, A., Sweetland, J., Wheeler, R., Minnici, A., & Carpenter, B. D. (2006). Preparing teachers for dialectically diverse classrooms. *Educational Researcher, 35,* 30–37.

Goldman, L. R. (1998). *Child's play: Myth, mimesis, and make-believe.* London: Routledge.

Gonzalez, N., Moll, L. C., & Amanti, C. (2005). Introduction: Theorizing practices. In N. Gonzalez, L. C. Moll, & C. Amanti (Eds.), *Funds of knowledge: Theorizing practices in households, communities, and classrooms* (pp. 1–28). Mahwah, NJ: Erlbaum.

Good, R. H., & Kaminski, R. A. (2002). *Dynamic Indicators of Basic Early Literacy Skills* (6th ed.). Eugene, OR: Institute for the Development of Educational Achievement.

Good Start, Grow Smart (2002). *The Bush administration's early childhood initiative.* Retrieved October 4, 2008, from: *http://www.whitehouse.gov/infocus/earlychildhood/earlychildhood.html*

Goodman, K. S. (2006). *The truth about DIBELS: What it is, what it does.* Portsmouth, NH: Heinemann.

Goodman, Y., & Goodman, D. (2000). "I hate 'postrophes": Issues of dialect and reading proficiency. In J. K. Peyton, P. Griffin, W. Wolfram, & R. Fasold (Eds.), *Language in action: New studies of language in society: Essays in honor of Roger W. Shuy* (pp. 408–35). Cresskill, NJ: Hampton Press.

Gould, S. J. (1996). *The mismeasure of man* (rev. ed.). New York: W. W. Norton.

Grant, R. A., Wong, S. D., & Osterling, J. P. (2007). Developing literacy in second-language learners: Critique from a heteroglossic, sociocultural, and multidimensional framework. *Reading Research Quarterly, 42*(4), 598–609.

Graue, M. E. (2006). The answer is readiness, now what is the question? *Early Education and Development, 17*(1), 43–56.

Greenfield, E., & Little, L. Jones. (1979). *Childtimes: A three-generation memoir.* New York: HarperCollins.

Grisham-Brown, J., Hemmeter, M. L., & Pretti-Frontczak, K. (2005). *Blended practices for teaching young children in inclusive settings.* Baltimore: Paul H. Brookes.

Gullo, D. (2005). *Understanding assessment and evaluation in early childhood education* (2nd ed.). New York: Teachers College Press.

Haight, L. (2002). *African American children at church: A sociocultural perspective.* New York: Cambridge University Press.

Halliday, M. A. K. (1975). *Learning how to mean: Explorations in the development of language.* London: Edward Arnold.

Hart, B., & Risley, T. (1995). *Meaningful differences in the everyday experience of young American children.* Baltimore: Paul H. Brookes.

Hartocollis, A. (2002, March 6). Boycotts and a bill protest mandatory state tests. Retrieved October 6, 2008, from: *New York Times Archives http://query.nytimes.com/gst/fullpage.html?res=9400E7DC1530F935A35750C0A9649C8B63&sec=&spon=&pagewanted=1*

Heath, S. B. (1983). *Ways with words: Language, life, and work in communities and classrooms.* Cambridge, United Kingdom: Cambridge University Press.

Helm, J. H., Beneke, S., & Steinheimer, K. (2007). *Windows on learning: Documenting young children's work.* New York: Teachers College Press.

Hernandez, D. J., Denton, N. A., Macartney, S. E. (2007). *Children in immigrant families— The United States and 50 states: National origins, language, and early education* (Publication 2007–11). Albany, NY: State University of New York Research Brief Series.

Hester, E. J. (1996). Narratives of young African American children. In A. Kamhi, K. E. Pollock, & J. L. Harris (Eds.), *Communication development and disorders in African American children* (pp. 227–246). Baltimore: Paul H. Brookes.

Hill, B. C. (2007). *Supporting your child's literacy learning.* Portsmouth, NH: Heinemann.

Hohmann, M., Banet, B., & Weikart, D. (1979). *Young children in action.* Ypsilanti, MI: High/Scope Press.

Hong, M. (2000). *We eat rice.* New York: Bebop.

Hong, M. (2001). *Teaching first grade: A practical guide.* New York: Scholastic.

Hu, W. (2008, August 6). Where the race now begins at kindergarten. *New York Times,* p. B-1.

"Humanities 101, Westfield style." (1992, March 3). *The Boston Globe,* p. 16.

Hyman, S. L., & Towbin, K. E. (2007). Autism spectrum disorders. In M. L. Batshaw, L. Pellegrino, & N. J. Roizen (Eds.), *Children with disabilities* (6th ed., pp. 326–343). Baltimore, MD: Paul H. Brookes.

Hymes, D. (1972). Models of the interaction of language and social life. In J. J. Gumperz & D. Hymes (Eds.), *Directions in sociolinguistics* (pp. 35–71). New York: Holt, Rinehart, & Winston.

Jablon, J. R., Dombro, A. L., & Dichtelmiller, M. L. (2007). *The power of observation for birth through eight* (2nd ed.). Washington, DC: National Association for the Education of Young Children.

Jenkins, H. (2006). *Convergence culture: Where old and new media collide.* New York: New York University Press.

Jones, B., & Hawes, B. L. (1972). *Step it down: Games, plays, songs, and stories from the Afro-American heritage.* New York: Harper & Row.

Kamler, B., & Comber, B. (Eds.). (2005). *Turn-around pedagogies: Literacy interventions for at-risk students.* Newtown, Australia: Primary English Teachers Association.

Kantor, H., & Lowe, R. (2006). From New Deal to no deal: No Child Left Behind and the devolution of responsibility for equal opportunity. *Harvard Educational Review, 76,* 474–502.

Karmiloff-Smith, A. (1986). Some fundamental aspects of language development after age 5. In P. Fletcher & M. Garman (Eds.), *Language acquisition* (2nd ed., pp. 455–474). New York: Cambridge University Press.

Keeves, J. A. (1994). Methods of assessment in schools. In T. Husen & T. N. Postlethwaite (Eds.), *The International Encyclopedia of Education* (2nd ed., vol. 1, p. 363). New York: Pergamon/Elsevier Science.

Kenner, C. (2004). *Becoming biliterate: Young children learning different writing systems.* Sterling, VA: Trentham Books.

Kenner, C. (2005). Bilingual children's uses of popular culture in text-making. In J. Marsh (Ed.), *Popular culture, new media, and digital literacy in early childhood* (pp. 73–88). London: Routledge.

Kightley, R. (1986). *Opposites.* Boston: Little Brown.

Kliewer, C., Fitzgerald, L. M., Meyer-Mork, J., Hartman, P., English-Sand, P. & Raschke, D. (2004). Citizenship for all in the literate community: An ethnography of young children with significant disabilities in inclusive early childhood settings. *Harvard Educational Review, 74*(4), 373–403.

Klima, E. S., & Bellugi-Klima, U. (1966). Syntactic regularities in the speech of children. In J. Lyons & R. J. Wales (Eds.), *Psycholinguistics: Papers* (pp. 183–208). Edinburgh: Edinburgh University Press.

Kohn, A. (2000). *The case against standardized testing: Raising the scores, ruining the schools.* Portsmouth, NH: Heinemann.

Kress, G. (2003). *Literacy in the new media age.* London: Routledge.

Labov, W. (1972). *Language in the inner city.* Philadelphia: University of Pennsylvania Press.

Ladson-Billings, G. (2001). *Crossing over to Canaan: The journey of new teachers in diverse classrooms.* San Francisco: Jossey-Bass.

Lancy, D. F. (2007). Accounting for variability in mother/child play. *American Anthropologist, 109,* 273–284.

Lareau, A. (2003). *Unequal childhoods: Class, race, and family life.* Los Angeles: University of California Press.

Lesko, N. (2001). *Act your age! A cultural construction of adolescence.* New York: Routledge.

Levin, I., & Bus, A. G. (2003). How is emergent writing based on drawing? Analyses of children's products and their sorting by children and mothers. *Developmental Psychology, 39,* 891–905.

Levine, R. (1997). *A geography of time: The temporal misadventures of a social psychologist, or how every culture keeps time just a little bit differently.* New York: Basic.

Levinson, M. (2007). Literacy in English Gypsy communities: Cultural capital manifested as negative assets. *American Educational Research Journal, 44,* 5–39.

Lindfors, J. W. (1999). *Children's inquiry: Using language to make sense of the world.* New York, NY: Teachers College Press.

Ling, M. (1992). *See how they grow: Butterfly.* New York: DK Preschool Publishing.

Love, A. M., Burns, S., & Buell, M. J. (2007). Writing: Empowering literacy. *Young Children, 62,* 13–19.

Lyotard, J.-F. (1984). *The postmodern condition: A report on knowledge.* Manchester, United Kingdom: Manchester University Press.

Marsh, J. (1999). Batman and Batwoman go to school: Popular culture in the literacy curriculum. *International Journal of Early Years Education, 7,* 117–131.

Marsh, J. (2003). Early childhood literacy and popular culture. In N. Hall, J. Larson, & J. Marsh (Eds.), *Handbook of early childhood literacy* (pp. 112–125). London: Sage.

Marsh, J. (2005). Moving stories: Digital editing in the nursery. In J. Evans (Ed.), *Literacy moves on: Using popular culture new technologies, and critical literacy in the primary classroom* (pp. 31–47). London: Fulton.

Marsh, J., & Millard, E. (2000). *Literacy and popular culture.* London: Sage.

Martin, B. (1983). *Brown bear, brown bear, what do you see?* New York: Henry Holt.

Matthews, J. (1999). *The art of childhood and adolescence: The construction of meaning.* London: Falmer Press.

McNaughton, C. (2002). *Meeting of minds.* Wellington, New Zealand: Learning Media Limited.

Mehan, H. (1979). *Learning lessons.* Cambridge, MA: Harvard University Press.

Meier, D., & Wood, G. (Eds.). (2004). *Many children left behind: How the No Child Left Behind Act is damaging our children and our schools.* Boston: Beacon Press.

Meier, T. (2008). *Black communications and learning to read.* New York: Erlbaum.

Meisels, S. J. (2002). *Thinking like a teacher: Using observational assessment to improve teaching and learning.* Boston: Allyn & Bacon.

Michaels, S. (1981). Sharing time: Children's narrative styles and differential access to literacy. *Language in Society, 10,* 423–442.

Miller, P. (1982). *Amy, Wendy, and Beth: Learning language in South Baltimore.* Austin: University of Texas Press.

Miller, P. (1996). Instantiating culture through discourse practices: Some personal reflections on socialization and how to study it. In R. Jessor, A. Colby, & R. Shweder (Eds.), *Ethnography and human development* (pp. 183–204). Chicago: University of Chicago Press.

Miller, P., & Goodnow, J. J. (1995). Cultural practices: Toward an integration of culture and development. In J. J. Goodnow, P. J. Miller, & F. Kessel (Eds.), *Cultural practices as contexts for development, No. 67, New directions in child development* (pp. 5–16). San Francisco: Jossey-Bass.

Moats, L. (2004). *Language essentials for teachers of reading and spelling.* Longmont, CO: Sopris West Educational Services.

Momaday, N. S. (1999). *In the bear's house.* New York: Harper Perennial.

NAEYC/NAECS/SDE (National Association for the Education of Young Children/National Association of Early Childhood Specialists in State Departments of Education). (2003). *Early childhood curriculum, assessment, and program evaluation: Building an effective, accountable system in programs for children birth through age 8.* Washington, DC: Authors.

National Center for Infants, Toddlers, and Families. (1997). *New visions for the developmental assessment of infants, toddlers, and families.* Washington, DC: Zero to Three.

National Commission on Excellence in Education. (*1983). A nation at risk.* Washington, DC: U. S. Department of Education.

Nelson, K. (1996). *Language in cognitive development: The emergence of the mediated mind.* Cambridge, United Kingdom: Cambridge University Press.

Nelson, K. (2007). *Young minds in social worlds: Experience, meaning, and memory.* Cambridge, MA: Harvard University Press.

Nichols, S. L., & Berliner, D. C. (2007). *Collateral damage: How high-stakes testing corrupts America's schools.* Cambridge, MA: Harvard Education Press.

Nieto, S. (2002). *Language, culture, and teaching critical perspectives for a new century.* Mahwah, NJ: Erlbaum.

No Child Left Behind Act of 2001. (2001). (PL 107–110). *www.ed.gov/nclb/landing.jhtml*

Ochs, E., & Capps, L. (2001). *Living narrative: Creating lives in everyday storytelling.* Cambridge, MA: Harvard University Press.

Ochs, E., & Schieffelin, B. B. (2001). Language acquisition and socialization: Three developmental stories and their implications. In A. Duranti (Ed.), *Linguistic Anthropology: A reader* (pp. 263–301). Malden, MA: Blackwell.

O'Neil, J. (2006, October 4). Early repairs in foundation for reading. *New York Times,* p. B9.

Pahl, K. (2003). Children's text making at home: Transforming meaning across modes. In C. Jewit & G. Kress (Eds.), *Multimodal literacy* (pp. 139–154). New York: Peter Lang.

Paley, V. G. (1997). *The girl with the brown crayon.* Cambridge, MA: Harvard University Press.

Paley, V. G. (2004). *A child's work: The importance of fantasy play.* Chicago: University of Chicago Press.

Paley, V. G. (2007a). Goldilocks and her sister: An anecdotal guide to the doll corner. *Harvard Educational Review 77*(2), 144–151.

Paley, V. G. (2007b). HER classic: On listening to what the children say. *Harvard Educational Review 77*(2), 152–163. Park, B. (1992–2005).

Percy, W. (1975). *Message in a bottle: How queer man is, how queer language is, and what one has to do with the other.* New York: Farrar, Straus.

Philips, S. (1972). Participant structures and communicative competence: Warm Springs children in community and classroom. In C. B. Cazden, V. P. John, & D. Hymes (Eds.), *Functions of language in the classroom* (pp. 370–394). New York: Teachers College Press.

Piaget, J. (2007). *The child's conception of time.* New York: Routledge Library Editions. (Original work published 1969)

Piestrup, A. (1973). *Black dialect interference and accommodation of reading instruction in first grade.* Berkeley, CA: University of California, Language-Behavior Research Laboratory.

Pinker, S. (1994). *The language instinct.* New York: William Morrow & Co.

Powell, D. R. (2005). The Head Start program. In J. L. Roopnarine & J. E. Johnson (Eds.), *Approaches to early childhood education* (4th ed., pp. 62–82). Upper Saddle River, NJ: Pearson.

Read, C. (1975). *Children's categorization of speech sounds in English.* Urbana, IL: National Council of Teachers of English.

Reyes, M. L. (2001). Unleashing possibilities: Biliteracy in the primary grades. In M. L. Reyes & J. J. Halcon (Eds.), *The best for our children: Critical perspectives on literacy for Latino students* (pp. 96–121). New York: Teachers College Press.

Richgels, D. (2001). Invented spelling, phonemic awareness, and reading and writing instruction. In S. B. Neuman & D. K. Dickinson (Eds.), *Handbook of early literacy research* (pp. 142–158). New York: Guildford.

Rickford, J. R. (1999). *African American Vernacular English: Features, evolution, educational implications.* Malden, MA: Blackwell Publishers.

Robinson, M., & Mackey, M. (2003). Film and television. In N. Hall, J. Larson, & J. Marsh (Eds.), *Handbook of early childhood literacy* (pp. 126–142). London: Sage.

Rogoff, B. (2003). *The cultural nature of human development.* New York: Oxford University Press.

Romaine, S. (1984). *The language of children and adolescents: The acquisition of communicative competence.* Oxford: Basil Blackwell.

Roskos, K., & Christie, J. F. (2001). *Play and literacy in early childhood: Research from multiple perspectives.* Mahwah, NJ: Erlbaum.

Samway, K. (2006). *When English language learners write: Connecting research to practice, K-8.* Portsmouth, NH: Heinemann.

Sarup, M. (1993). *An introductory guide to post-structuralism and postmodernism* (2nd ed.). New York: Longman.

Scharer, P. L., & Zutell, J. (2003). The development of spelling. In N. Hall, J. Larson & J. Marsh (Eds.), *Handbook of early childhood literacy* (pp. 271–286). London: Sage.

Schweinhart, L. J., & Weikart, D. P. (1997). The High/Scope preschool curriculum comparison study through age 23. *Early Childhood Research Quarterly, 12,* 117–143.

Scott, J. (1998). The serious side of Ebonics humor. *Journal of English Linguistics, 26,* 137–155.

Serna, I. A., & Hudelson, S. (1993). Emergent Spanish literacy in a Whole Language bilingual classroom. In R. Donmoyer & R. Kos (Eds.), *At-risk students: Portraits policies programs and practices* (pp. 291–321). Albany: State University of New York Press.

Seymour, H. N., & Roeper, T. (1999). Grammatical acquisition of African American English. In O. Taylor & L. Leonard (Eds.), *Language acquisition across North America* (pp. 109–153). San Diego: Singular.

Shepard, L. (1999). Promotion and retention. In J. P. Heubert & R. M. Hauser (Eds.), *High stakes testing for tracking, promotion, and graduation.* Washington, DC: National Academy Press. Chapter 6 only, on Promotion and Retention may be downloaded from *http://books.nap.edu/books/0309062802/html/114.html*

Shepard, L. (2006). Classroom assessment. In R. L. Brennan (Ed.), *Educational measurement* (4th ed., pp. 623–646). Westport, CT: American Council on Education/Praeger.

Sims, R. (1976). What we know about dialects and reading. In P. D. Allen & D. J. Watson (Eds.), *Findings of research in miscue analysis: Classroom implications* (pp. 128–131). Urbana, IL: NCTE.

Singer, D. G., Golinkoff, R. M., & Hirsh-Pasek, K. (Eds.). (2006). *Play = learning.* New York: Oxford University Press.

Skinner, B. F. (1957). *Verbal behavior.* New York: Appleton-Century-Crofts.

Smith, R. C. (2006). *Mexican New York: Transnational lives of new immigrants.* Berkeley: University of California Press.

Smith, Z. (2000). *White teeth: A novel.* New York: Vintage.

Smitherman, G. (1977). *Talkin and testifyin: The language of Black America.* Boston: Houghton Mifflin.

Smitherman, G. (1994). *Black talk: Words and phrases from the hood to the Amen Corner.* Boston: Houghton Mifflin.

Smitherman, G. (2006). *Word from the mother: Language and African Americans.* New York: Routledge.

Sowell, T. (1997). *Late-talking children.* New York: Basic.

Stetsenko, A. (1995). The psychological function of children's drawing: A Vygotskian perspective.

In C. Lange-Kuttner & G. V. Thomas (Eds.), *Drawing and looking: Theoretical approaches to pictorial representation in children* (pp. 147–158). New York: Harvester/Wheatsheaf.

Stevens, S. (2007). Introduction: How I trumped Rudolf Steiner and overcame the tribulations of illiteracy, one Snickers bar at a time. In D. Eggers (Ed.), *The best American nonrequired reading, 2007* (pp. xi–xviii). Boston: Houghton Mifflin.

Stires, S. (2002). *Building another world: Three first graders' learning of English language and literacy in school.* Unpublished doctoral dissertation. Teachers College, New York.

Stires, S., & Genishi, C. (2008). Learning English in school: Rethinking curriculum. In C. Genishi, & A. L. Goodwin (Eds.), *Diversities in early childhood education: Rethinking and doing* (pp. 49–66). New York: Routledge.

Stracher, C. (1999, April 15). Rejection at an early age. *New York Times,* p. A31.

Street, B. V. (Ed.). (1993). *Cross-cultural approaches to literacy.* Cambridge, United Kingdom: Cambridge University Press.

Strickland, D. (1998). *Teaching phonics today: A primer for educators.* Newark, DE: International Reading Association.

Tabors, P. O. (1997). *One child, two languages.* Baltimore: Paul H. Brookes.

Thorndike, R. L., & Hagen, E. P. (1977). *Measurement and evaluation in psychology and education* (4th ed.). New York: Wiley.

U. S. Department of Education. (2004). Individuals with disabilities act of 2004. Retrieved January 4, 2009, from *http://idea.ed.gov*

Van Hoorn, J. L., Nourot, P., Scales, B., & Alward, M. C. (2006). *Play at the center of the curriculum* (4th ed.). Upper Saddle River, NJ: Pearson.

Vasquez, O., Pease-Alvarez, L., & Shannon, S. M. (1994). *Pushing boundaries: Language and culture in a Mexicano community.* New York: Cambridge University Press.

Voices Inside Schools. (2007). Special issue of *Harvard Educational Review 77*(2).

Vygotsky, L. S. (1962). *Thought and language.* Cambridge, MA: MIT Press.

Vygotsky, L. S. (1978). *Mind in society.* Cambridge, MA: Harvard University Press.

Vygotsky, L. S. (1987). *L. S. Vygotsky, collected works: Volume 1, Problems of general psychology.* New York: Plenum Books.

Waters, J., Frantz, J. F., Rottmayer, S., Trickett, M., & Genishi, C. (1992). Learning to see the learning of preschool children. In C. Genishi (Ed.), *Ways of assessing children and curriculum: Stories of early childhood practice* (pp. 25–57). New York: Teachers College Press.

Williams, T., & Feldman, C. (2007, July 1). Stickball anyone? In a PlayStation world, maybe not. *The New York Times,* p. 21.

Witte, S. (1992). Context, text, and intertext: Toward a constructivist semiotic of writing. *Written Communication, 9,* 313–341.

Wolfram, W., C. T. Adger, & Christian, D. (1999). *Dialects in schools and communities.* Mahwah, NJ: Erlbaum.

Wolfson, N. (1982). *CHP, the conversational historical present in American English narrative.* Dordrecht, Holland: Foris Publications.

Wurm, J. (2005). *Working in the Reggio way: A beginners' guide for American teachers.* St. Paul, MN: Redleaf.

Yamamoto, K. (1979). *Children in time and space.* New York: Teachers College Press.

Youssef, V. (1993). Children's linguistic choice: Audience design and societal norms. *Language in Society, 22,* 257–274.

Zager, D. (2004). *Autism spectrum disorders: Identification, education, and treatment* (3rd ed.). Mahwah, NJ: Erlbaum.

Index

About the Authors

Celia Genishi, a former secondary Spanish and preschool teacher, is professor of education and chair of the department of curriculum and teaching at Teachers College, Columbia University. She teaches courses related to early childhood education and qualitative research methods. Previously she was on the faculty at the University of Texas at Austin and the Ohio State University. The editor of *Ways of Assessing Children and Curriculum: Stories of Early Childhood Practice,* she is coauthor (with Millie Almy) of *Ways of Studying Children.* Her research interests include collaborative research with teachers, childhood bilingualism, and children's language use in classrooms. She is gratified to be a recipient of the Advocate for Justice Award from the American Association of Colleges for Teacher Education.

Anne Haas Dyson is a former teacher of young children and, currently, a professor of education at the University of Illinois at Urbana-Champaign. Previously she was on the faculty of the University of Georgia, Michigan State University, and the University of California, Berkeley, where she was a recipient of the campus Distinguished Teaching Award. She studies the childhood cultures and literacy learning of young schoolchildren. Among her publications are *Social Worlds of Children Learning to Write in an Urban Primary School,* which was awarded NCTE's David Russell Award for Distinguished Research; *Writing Superheroes: Contemporary Childhood, Popular Culture, and Classroom Literacy;* and *The Brothers and Sisters Learn to Write: Popular Literacies in Childhood and School Cultures.*

Together **Celia Genishi** and **Anne Haas Dyson** have collaborated on a number of publications, among them *Language Assessment in the Early Years* (1984), *The Need for Story: Cultural Diversity in Classroom and Community* (1994), and *On the Case: Approaches to Language and Literacy Research* (2005).